ACTIVATE

Unorthodox philosophies that explore anxiety, depression, and suicidal thoughts as symptoms of suppressed superpower

By

Timmésha Burgess

Copyright © 2021 by Timmésha Burgess M.Sc., Psychology. All rights reserved.

All rights reserved. No part of this book may be produced by any mechanical, photographic, or electronic process, or in the form of a phonographic recording; nor may it be stored in a retrieval system, transmitted, or otherwise be copied for public or private use— or other than for "fair use" as brief quotations embodied in articles and reviews— without prior written permission of the publisher. The author of this book does not dispense medical advice or prescribe the use of any technique as a form of treatment for physical, emotional, or medical problems without the advice of a physician, either directly or indirectly. The intent of the author is only to offer information of a general nature to help you in your quest for mental, emotional, and spiritual well-being. In the event you use any of the information in this book for yourself, the author and the publisher assume no responsibility for your actions.

Note: The case studies found in this book are composite drawn from years of spiritual work and new ideals obtained on my personal mental health journey. These concepts are true to the spirit of ancient wisdom and knowledge.

The time is up for awakening. It's now time to ACTIVATE. Awakening was the phase when we opened our eyes, and activation is where we rise. Now go forth, and continue to evolve, having fully activated all of your ancient superpowers in integrity and in (no-longer-hidden other) truth.

Disclaimer: This work is not intended to substitute for professional medical or counseling advice, but to couple it. The concepts shared here are also advice and theory, just as medical perspectives have derived their theories over time via what clinical professionals call "medical practice." However, if you suffer from an otherwise physical or mental illness, please seek medical advice.

CONTENTS

Introduction 7

Chapter 1: Mental Disorders Throughout the Ages 9

   Mental disorder vs. mental illness 18

Chapter 2: Mental Disorders & Sexual Trauma 43

   Jezebel Speaks 43

   The Istanbul Convention 51

Chapter 3: Mental Disorders & Suppressed Feminine Power ... 72

Chapter 4: Mental Disorders & The Alchemical Process 98

   Twilight 124

   Dusk 128

   Dawn 146

Chapter 5: Mental Disorders & The Chosen Ones 170

   Contemplate suicide or have thoughts death (suicidal ideation) 191

Chapter 6: Lose Your Mind for Better Mental Health 202

Diagnostic Statistical Manual- Activated (DSM-A) 207

   Anxiety Redefined 208

   Depression Redefined 220

Activate Glossary 235

Acknowledgements 237

About the Author 241

References 243

ACTIVATE

Unorthodox philosophies that explore anxiety, depression, and suicidal thoughts as symptoms of suppressed superpower

INTRODUCTION

I hold a bachelor's degree in sociology and a master's in psychology, but none of my degrees prepared me for life's lessons on the true nature of mental disorders, which ran contrary to everything I was ever taught. In order to bridge the gap between mental health disorders and suppressed superpowers; I dared to explore the correlation of the witch hunts between the 16th and 18th century, religious doctrine, demonology, and cultural beliefs to the beginning of when I believe the onset of mental disorders began. I attribute the ancient wisdom and knowledge shared here to my own personal journey through my dark night of the soul, sacred teachings and methodologies, ancestral guidance, and to the inspirational works and research of Swiss psychiatrist and psychoanalyst Dr. Carl Jung. During my undergraduate and graduate careers, none of my professors deeply explored the realms of Jungian theory. Only the usual route from Freud to Pavlov, Rogers, and the likes of those that were led purely by what they could see as opposed to what they could not see. I mention this because the information in this book is purely based on what we call "the unseen" and the uncharted—taboo aspects of mental health considered weird, strange, and unexplainable by modern science. These ideas are kept hidden in the dark and swept under the rugs of traditional approaches. Freud merely shared his own theories about the psychological state of a person, right? Why can't those of us that have actually taken the journey through the darkness of mental health do the same? This book presents "other-side-of-the-door" perspectives on mental health disorders, because it defies the norm and explores the shadows of what's typically masked in clinical mental health approaches. If you or someone you know does not, cannot, or has not, responded to traditional mental health approaches geared to combat anxiety, depression, and suicidal thoughts, then this is the book for you! The contents of this manual are universally adoptable for and by both women and men. Please keep in mind that every person on this planet and beyond is made up of **both** feminine and masculine energies; therefore, if you are a male reading this do not be dismayed by its contents. In my personal quest to serve women and girls (ages 13 or older) affected by mental disorders such as anxiety, depression, and thoughts of suicide; I also discovered that a large part of mental health issues that occur in men is due to the continuous suppression of their own feminine power and energy. Before beginning this written work, I had a dream one year prior. In the dream I along with two others guiding me, accessed a locked room with a key. The room was filled with files, folders, and documents. Two others with me and I sat down, and opened a briefcase; inside were documents. We began reading the pages of this one document, and one of the people guiding me (a male) said, "**This is going to be one of the most powerful books ever written.**" At the time I had NO IDEA that I would ever decide to write a book; in fact, I would often say that I prefer to write articles because they are shorter and quicker to read. It appears that something greater had other plans for me, because through me this work is being produced, a work much more profound than I could have even imagined would be happening through me. After being taken on a startling, dark, and mystical journey to discover exactly what anxiety, depression, and suicidal thoughts were for me and so many others, here I am writing or dare I say, activating one of the most powerful books ever written. A written work that explores **witch hunts**, **demonology**, and our overall concept of **hell** as the sources of misunderstood, misused, and abused superpower. A power so deeply suppressed due to trauma, taught beliefs, and false doctrine that it now shows up in almost every man, woman, and child on the planet as mental health disorders.

Timmesha Burgess

CHAPTER 1: MENTAL DISORDERS THROUGHOUT THE AGES

In order to reveal the powerful, life-shifting, mind-altering unorthodox philosophies regarding anxiety, depression, and suicidal thoughts; I've had to dive and dig in deep! So deep in fact, that I was led to travel back in time to a place that still haunts society today— a time on our planet that will forever and always be remembered as **The Witch Trials.**

I've had and continue to have ***ah-ha*** moments, in which deep revelations arise regarding when, where, why, and how something happens, such as when I first realized (or saw with my "real- eye" i.e., third eye) that based on all that I share in this book, I would have been and still would be considered a witch, why? Because I possess abilities that few understand and that many consider to be of "The Devil" (pause for dramatic effect). But one revelation in particular struck a chord.

It came as I watched a TV series called **Penny Dreadful**, a story that takes place between the 18th and 19th-centuries. In one episode of this critically acclaimed Netflix thriller/horror series, a character named Vanessa visits a known witch's home on the outskirts of the rural lands. Vanessa is in search of the one woman that she believes can help her understand who she is, and why she is being tormented by the devil. The witch is not so welcoming to her; In fact, she too has experienced extreme loss and betrayal from those closest to her so it's hard for her to trust anyone. The townspeople called the witch "The Cut Wife." This meant that the witch is known and judged for performing what she called, "***cuttin babies outta girls that got nowhere else to go***," which today is commonly known as abortion. When the witch realizes that Vanessa refuses to give up hope, the witch eventually lets her pass the protection shield she set to keep out untrue spirits.

Activate

We learn through Vanessa's encounter with the witch that many women and girls have come to her who've been raped by men, mentally, or sexually controlled by their husbands. And though the enforcement of sexual acts were considered solely responsible for unwanted pregnancies, females shouldered all the blame. Vanessa's reason for visiting is not all that different, and after the interaction we see each of them go on their way while we sit in abhorrence of the way many women and girls have been historically treated. However, the story doesn't let us continue in that true but narrow way of thought for long.

To make a long story short, the witch performs the abortion while the girl is sobbing, and the girl goes on her way. In the meantime, one of the witch's sisters from a former coven was planning to betray the witch because the coven wanted to take Vanessa and give her to Satan. In fact, there was a scene where the same girl that was there for an abortion, was the same girl that yelled, "*Burn the witch*," during a townhall meeting. Although the people were all manipulated by spell work to turn against the witch, it was a true testament to the betrayal common among women, sisters, wives, and friends—who instead of protecting each other, choose to inflict pain on each other. Why? Simply put: **Fear, Competition, Jealousy, and Hate**! In fact, most of the townspeople had secretly gone to the witch for some sort of help, yet, in turn, plotted against her in secret. It was easy for the young girl, although under spell work, to turn against the witch because of her own fear that others would find out she too had been there for an abortion. So, instead of being found out and facing that judgement from others, it'd be better for the witch to burn. The women of the former coven hate the former witch. Why? Because she chooses not to use alchemy to purposely harm others via death rituals, beauty spells to make her look younger by bathing in the blood of a murdered newborn, and human sacrifices (although she had the power to). She instead chooses to live (in a sense) more righteous and independent, and this infuriates the former coven.

The townspeople along with her former coven all arrive at the witch's house, drug her outside, beat her, tie her to a tree, pour hot tar on her, and set her on fire. In fact, the young girl that received an abortion from the witch a few nights prior is *the first* one to set the flame, by placing a lit torch to her body. The witch never blinks an eye or utters a peep. She stands firm in the power of who she is as her own type of healer—even when those she once helped, and whose lives she once saved, stand privately for her but publicly against her. But we are given a larger lens here, because in the final season of this show, the witch reincarnates as one of the most high-profiled therapists in the world—who just so happens to specialize in rare spiritual cases—and Vanessa is recommended as one her clients. Oh the irony of unfinished works being done and wrongs being righted, no matter how many lifetimes it takes.

Why do I share these examples from the Netflix series *Penny Dreadful* as it relates to mental health disorders throughout the ages? For starters, these depictions for me highlight four (4) key components to the development of anxiety and depression in women perpetuated throughout lifetimes;

1. **Ongoing generational, psychological curses develop on the premise that if you're talented, empathic, gifted, a healer, or have natural abilities, you are an evil threat and are a "witch."**

Below is a direct quote from **Rehabilitating the Witch:** *The Literary Representation of the Witch from the Malleus Maleficarum to Les Enfants du sabbat,* by Lisa Travis Blomquist, that expresses the rise, fall, and rebirth of the misinterpretation of the title of witches.

Activate

> The representation of the witch in French literature has evolved considerably over the centuries. While originally portrayed as a benevolent and caring healer in works by Marie de France, Chretien de Troyes, and the anonymous author of *Amadas et Ydoine*, the witch eventually underwent a dramatic and unfortunate transformation. By the fifteenth century, authors began to portray her as a malevolent and dangerous agent of the Christian Devil. Martin Le Franc, Pierre de Ronsard, Joachim du Bellay, Francois Rabelais, and Pierre Comeille all created evil witch figures that corresponded with this new definition. It was not until the eighteenth century, through the works of Voltaire and the Encyclopedistes, that the rehabilitation of the witch began. By the twentieth century, Anne Hebert, Jean-Paul Sartre, Maryse Conde, and Sebastiano Vassalli began to rewrite the witch character by engaging in a process of demystification and by demonstrating that the "witch" was really just a victim of the society in which she lived (Blomquist, 2).

I included the passage above because it is important to note that the term witch originally derived from a place of honor and respect alluding to the people that offered their natural abilities through the practice of healing arts. However, throughout time, being called a witch became a derogatory term that carried the weight of wickedness and evil works. But why, and how does this affect us today?

Based on my research, and from what I was directly channeled, downloaded, uploaded from my spirit/invisible guides, and by doing the inner work to re-awaken and activate an ancient knowledge within me, it had been made evident to me that anything that is light has an equal and as powerful counterpart that is dark or of the shadows. This is what we call the balance of life. Yes! People allowed their *inactivated unawaken, and unrefined* minds and emotions to rule their decisions so much so, that it got in the way of their spiritual gifts. What began as a way to **heal, uplift,** and **empower** quickly turned into a tool to **kill, steal,** and **destroy.** Both women (and men) began to use the power of alchemy to hurt and overpower others, as in the case of the women from the former coven in *Penny Dreadful.*

There also existed those who falsely accused women of performing evil acts, just because he wanted her and she refused him; or by claiming that "**she was from the devil who made me do it**," when allegations of cheating on a spouse were made. Egos spewed malice as those who felt rejected by beautiful and powerful women, sought criminal claims against the ones they wanted and knew they couldn't have, or on the premise of not wanting to take the blame for being caught in the act of what many call "adultery" and fornication. This became truer due to living during a time when the church was the judge, jury, and executioner. Witch hunts murdered hundreds of *innocent* women, many of which were in the practice of offering their own healing modalities with the application of homemade, natural, herbal remedies. Many of the murders were never reported, so no one really knows the number of crimes committed against **women-alchemists** who were actually performing "good works."

According to Blomquist:

> While occasional men were accused and convicted of witchcraft during this fatal craze, the witch was envisioned primarily as a female, with men implicated most often for merely being related by birth or marriage

to women who had themselves been found accused of witchcraft. According to some reports, women made up eighty to eighty-five percent of those executed for witchcraft, and were accused, convicted, and executed, in comparison to men, at a ratio of about four to one. It is no wonder that many feminist scholars have referred to witchcraft persecutions as "holocausts of women" and as "women hunting." And it is no wonder that the modem image of the witch remains almost always female (Blomquist, 8-9).

The fear of being killed was ingrained in the psyche and energetic bodies of the descendants left behind by those murdered women. Even if they didn't know their ancestral history per se, the energetic fear of pain carried over into their bloodlines and perpetuated itself generation after generation. Those girls grew to become women that gave birth to other women and men, who also carried the same energetic curse of fearing for their lives. Witch hunts (i.e., crimes against women) presented itself as a ploy against unique women, one that aimed to scare any source of the *feminine* into submission and servitude to the *masculine*. And boy did it work! Due to the need to stay alive, survive, and protect themselves and their families from attack, women who embodied the energy to heal were forced into hiding or murdered. Among the many reasons, this was why, when, where, and how women began to hide, suppress, and learned to vilify their inner-alchemical power in the early ages. This cycle continues to this day; a power suppressed for so many lifetimes, that it now shows up as *anxiety, depression*, and *suicidal ideation*.

2. **When you display abilities that others haven't or don't take the time to cultivate within themselves; you are considered "the unusual/weird" outsider.**

In the witch's and Vanessa's case, they were aliens in a world that both loved them for their gifts and hated them for the same. Anxiety, depression, and thoughts of dying are symptoms expressed in those that are deemed the weird ones; however, they are also the ones with deep spiritual gifts. Unfortunately, derogatory terms projected by those who have not yet developed their own spiritual gifts causes the ones who are already "born with it" to hide and mask their true selves, thus perpetuating the continued expression of what looks like a mental health disorder.

3. Women began to oppress one another long before *certain* men ever could!

Wondering why I italicized "certain"? Well, because it wasn't every man on the planet that felt intimidated by women alchemists. In fact, there were men (who themselves practiced the art of alchemy, labeled "wiccans") that attempted to protect these women, and they were also murdered and/or outcast as a result. Frankly speaking, the rise against women in their power was LARGELY due to women who had not yet come into their own **balanced power** (*an even distribution of weight enabling someone or something to remain upright and steady; a state in which different things occur in equal or proper amounts or have an equal or proper amount of importance*); due to this lack of mental stability these women only grew jealous, angry, and intimidated by the women who did.

In the witch's case, her coven turned against her because she refused to purposely attack and target others for selfish gain. What is this phenomenon of women turning against other women in which today's society calls hating, gang-stalking, and back-biting? This phenomenon is now known as **mental and emotional instability**, **imbalance**, or **improper use** or **abuse of power**.

Activate

As I mentioned in #1 above, "***people allowed their untrained, unawaken, and inactivated, and unrefined minds and emotions to rule their decisions, so much so that it got in the way of their spiritual gifts. What began as a way to heal, uplift, and empower quickly turned into a tool to kill, steal, and destroy. Both women (and men) began to use the power of alchemy to hurt and attempt to overpower others.***"

For instance, in *Penny Dreadful,* the witch of the coven that wanted to take Vanessa to Satan used her sexual prowess like a spell and conjured spells using totems, as a way to entice a local politician, whom she just so happened to be dating. She began dating him just so she could use him to hang the witch protecting Vanessa. One night, she went to his home (invited by him), and performed for him in the manner in which he liked. By doing so, she was able to convince him that the witch needed to hang for crimes she did not commit. While atop him she whispered in his ear saying, "***You must charge her of these crimes, you wouldn't want the people of this town to see you as weak now would you?***" I share this scene from this series to paint the example of how unbalanced, misused, and abused sexual and sensual energy can and has been used to perpetuate bloodshed and wars throughout centuries. A simple play on the ego by someone who has not developed mental health nor emotional health can spew a whirlwind of chaos. There existed (and still exists) women who indeed practice the art of seduction and were highly revered for their ability to arouse men near and far. However, this art was only practiced by shaman-like figures who resided in temples and only worked in the practice as a healing modality.

The art of sexuality, sensuality, and seduction stem from ancient practices of raising the heat of the loins (Kundalini fire), *only* so that it can be channeled into other parts of the body for healing terminal illnesses. However, in the wrong hands and hearts, this art became degraded by those that carried ill motives. Many mentally and emotionally unstable women (and men), began to *knowingly use* their sexual energies as a weapon, not to end wars but to begin them. According to the ***Activate*** philosophy, this act of treachery is no longer classified as a mental disorder, but as **mental illness**.

Contrary to traditional medical definitions that clump mental disorder and mental illness together, mental illness and mental disorder are categorically different according to this body of work, although terms are often used interchangeably. But here is why they are different. When a person *purposely* and *knowingly* chooses not to raise their power for complete activation, mental illness (toxicity) is the result. A sickness fueled by chaos and confusion in those who seek to cause harm to others, without probable cause other than their own jealousy and hate. In this case and in my personal opinion, mental disorders are vastly different in *nature* from mental illnesses. In my search to find compelling evidence that suggests the difference between mental disorder and mental illness, I was met with disappointment in the fact that clinical research hasn't done a better job at clarifying the distinct differences between the two. In fact, one report stated by the National Alliance on Mental Illness (NAMI) states, "**NAMI recognizes that other organizations have drawn distinctions between what diagnoses are considered 'mental health conditions' as opposed to 'mental illnesses.' We intentionally use the terms 'mental health conditions' and 'mental illness/es' interchangeably.**" This statement solidifies one thing for me, and that's the fact that some get it and some don't. Meaning, those who have dared to dive deeper into clarifying the differences, "over"stand the need to establish concrete boundaries between nature vs. nurture. "**A disorder is characterized by functional impairment and a disruption to the body's normal function and structure**" (Verywellhealth.com).

Activate

The ***Activate*** philosophy suggests that a mental disorder is impaired function, not an illness often measured by bacteria or virus in the body. These distinctions are proof of **knowledge and wisdom that can be activated to heal, uplift, and build nations that are *out of order* (out of place or stuck in one place) in the mind and body.** As it relates to the above definition of disorder, one can ascertain that for those on this journey of exploring anxiety, depression, and suicidal thoughts as symptoms of suppressed superpower, that functional impairment and disruption to the body's normal function and structure is due to the *disruption of individual power*. However, mental illness displays itself as toxic-like traits within the person that says, "*I know* **I can raise my power up to help and heal, but I'd rather use it to kill, and destroy.**" Mental illness acts as a disease of the mind that spreads throughout the body as dangerous emotions that may purposely seek destruction. Mental illness may be medically plausible as disease or bacteria that show up as a virus in the body in those who suffer from bipolar disorder and schizophrenia. However, mental disorder cannot be measured because it is an unseen battle invisible to blood tests. You won't see mental disorders such as anxiety, depression, and thoughts of suicide particularly show up as a virus or bacteria in the body, because this phenomenon is on a spiritual level which cannot be measured by medicine alone. In a nutshell, mental illness and mental disorder differ much like that of the **hunter** and the **hunted**.

MENTAL DISORDER VS. MENTAL ILLNESS

To delve deeper into the difference between **mental disorder** vs. **mental illness**, I will allow my intuitive ancient self to speak through me. Throughout this book I will embed a number of my intuitively led messages that are *downloaded, uploaded*, and *activated* through me to give you the reader, deeper insight into a particular point. Only when I'm guided to do so. These messages will at times come across raw and unfiltered. But, I can only share the messages with you as they are activated within me, so here goes.

> **Downloaded/Uploaded/ Intuitively Channeled Message**
>
> The powers that have been suppressed within you show up as anxiety and depression, this is what you call disorder. This disorder means that your power is out of its correct order and place, therefore, you are confused about who and what you are. However, those that seek to harm others do so not because they suffer from disorder, but because they have purposely chosen to unleash their power specifically to cause chaos. This is a sickness that spreads throughout the mind and emotions of the *oppressor,* hence mental illness. You that are experiencing anxiety, depression, and suicidal thoughts, however, are neither ill nor sick, but merely experiencing the symptoms of displaced power. Power that is out of order, out of place inside you—hence, "dis-order." Mental illness hunts for power by attempting to misuse, abuse, and usurp it from others; while mental disorder seeks to re-order its "out-of-order" power for the purpose of healing and uplifting. For these reasons, you who are experiencing mental disorders are often the ones hunted. Those who perpetuate their mental illness seek to hunt, but those with mental disorders are the hunted. You are easy prey because you have not yet activated your own power.
>
> **—The Ancients, The All Knowing**

Because of the *lower activation* of these powers, there have been a number of women who indeed have attempted to use the power of alchemy to attack others with what are called "**spells.**" Mental illness (a sickness) drives the mind and heart of those who become intimidated by others who are naturally born with their power. This means that some are born DNA coded with gifts so profound that it has the ability to heal nations; while some seek to gather their power by usurping it from others through treacherous acts. In this case, it is no longer the alchemy of pain to power, but power into pain.

According to Wikipedia, spells are defined as,

> An incantation, a spell, a charm, an enchantment or a bewitchery, is a magical formula intended to trigger a magical effect on a person or objects. The formula can be spoken, sung or chanted. An incantation can also be performed during ceremonial rituals or prayers. In the world of magic, incantations are said to be performed by wizards, witches, and fairies. In medieval literature, folklore, fairy tales, and modern fantasy fiction, enchantments are charms or spells. This has led to the terms "enchanter" and "enchantress" for those who use enchantments. The term was loaned into English around AD 1300. The corresponding native English term being "galdr" "song, spell." The weakened sense "delight" (compare the same development of "charm") is modern, first attested in 1593 (OED). Surviving written records of historical magic spells were largely obliterated in many cultures by the success of the major monotheistic religions (Islam, Judaism, and Christianity), which label *some magical activity as immoral or associated with evil.*

I purposely italicized the last portion of the last sentence because I want to be clear that alchemical processes have, can be, and still are used for reasons that are immorally fucked up! [*Clears throat*], or should I say lowly activated. Now I'm not going to go into full detail about incantations, so on and so forth, because if you're reading this book then you are already aware of these concepts. However, I want to share a truth-moment with you, as it relates to my own personal experience of being on the receiving end of what we call spells or spell work attacks.

Truth Moment: Early 2020, my sister-in-law and I were chatting one day about all things other worldly, meditation, and family. She then looked at me and said, "*I know you protect this house because I've seen all types of things I've never seen before.*" I asked her like what? She said, "*Well, the energy I feel when you meditate is so overwhelming I feel like I want to cry, and from the knife in the front yard behind the bush—*" I stopped her immediately, and asked, "*What knife?*" She said, "*The one behind the bush... there's like a knife with an old wooden handle ... like an old steak knife behind the bush.*" I immediately went to check and there it was, a knife with a wooden handle that resembled an old steak knife; stabbed perfectly into the ground directly in-front of my living rooms bay window.

As soon as I saw it, a flood of visions poured into my mind's eye showing me a person or people in the middle of the night, who came and plunged the knife into the ground right outside of my living room bay window. According to what many understand as spiritual wisdom; the home represents the body and the position of the knife according to ancient ritualistic practices, symbolizes driving a knife into someone's back. I began to feel the angst of when our ancestors would be awakened in the middle of the night to a burning cross, hanging dead animals, and dolls with knives stuck in them in their front yard. I often wondered what would drive a person to go to such lengths to harm another by way of spell work. Frankly speaking, the only explanation is the projection of their own fear that someone else may be, look, speak, walk, and talk differently than them. And by different, I mean their own belief that someone else is "greater than me." I removed the knife with a white handkerchief, poured some pure red dirt I picked up from my local crystal store on the spot, and burned a white candle at my outside window seal until it burned out. I then drove to a river with one of my dear mentor friends who's in her early seventies, and I recited these words aloud: "**All that was sent to hurt, harm, kill, destroy, and steal from me I send back to senders instantly. I send their gifts back wrapped in immovable, unbreakable, unshakable love**." Then I tossed the knife into the rushing river. Why did I send it back wrapped with love when their intentions were so full of malice? Because, there is no stronger force than love. My higher self knew that when I sent all they sent back to them, that they would never be able to give away what they tried to send me and no one would be able to take it away from them, because of the impenetrable force of love. They would be forever bound to that which they not only attempted to send to me but that which they attempted to do to others. As soon as I released the knife, I immediately felt an energetic shift so much so that force of the winds picked up.

Prior to the discovery of this knife, my car had been broken into for a second time. The first time that my car had been broken into, the assailant gathered all of the items in my car and placed them in a pile in the middle of the road. I know, this because when I awoke to see that my car door was ajar and that things were scattered all over my seat, I asked a neighbor if she saw anyone. Her response: "**I saw a pile of all women's stuff sitting nice and neat in the middle of the road and people were just driving over it. I thought that someone's stuff was being put out because it just looked like someone just neatly set it there, but now I see that was your stuff. Wow, that's strange to do if they didn't actually take anything!**"

I share these attempts at spell work that were meant to harm and even KILL me, to paint the picture of the degree in which power may be misused and abused by those with mental illness. The cars driving over my personal items was indicative of people running over me and trampling me to the ground. The intent was for me to attract the energy of worthlessness, helplessness, defeat, and death. Consider those who hold high level positions within our world, or those who speak out against injustices. If you ask them, I can absolutely guarantee that they would have stories for days about those who threatened to take their life, and those who have actually attempted to do so through the act of spell casting.

Photos of knife used as a spell.

End of truth moment

So, wondering how it's possible to conduct spells in order to attack others with the misuse and abuse of sexual energy? Allow me to give you a visual representation of *what, where,* and *how* unbalanced, unintelligent, and *unrefined* power remains stuck in the lower body, and how this energy may be used as a weapon via spell work by those with mental illness (*not mental disorder, please remember Activates difference between the two previously mentioned*), when not properly activated.

The diagram below shows a picture of our inner chakra systems that house and allocate energy throughout our bodies.

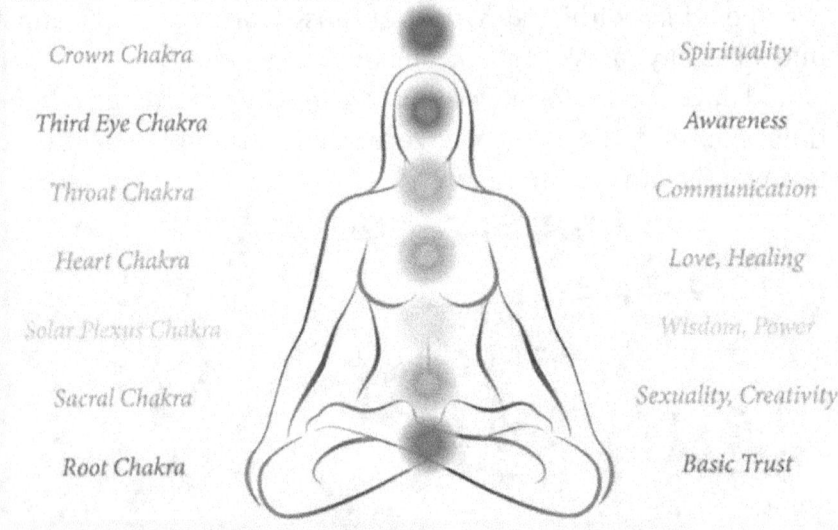

Photo taken from Chakra Anatomy (chakra-anatomy.com)

Take notice of the two lowest chakra centers which are the root chakra (red) and the sacral chakra (orange). These *lower-level* chakras house both our sensual and sexual energies in the areas of our vaginas and our wombs. When these chakra centers are misused and abused (i.e., not alchemically activated), it can create mental disorder or illness/disease depending on the person over time. Those who specifically suffer from **mental illness/disease,** who purposely choose to wield power from these lower chakra centers without first having *raised for activation*, will exhibit some or more of the following;

- Outbursts of anger and rage in an attempt to overpower those they feel threatened by

- Will display attachments to people, places, and things based on their desire for control
- Present themselves as honorable *only* when in the presence of those they wish to impress
- Will use sex as a tool to attach others (sex as a weapon)
- Will attempt to manipulate the decisions, situations, and outcomes of others for personal gain through bullying, lying, and deceit
- Will conspire and be drawn to gossip, chaotic or dramatic situations
- Will attempt to gain power from others through slander, hate, and toxic competition due to feeling powerless

By choosing to operate solely and purposely out of the lower chakra areas keeps power stagnant, stuck in the lower base centers of the body, causing continued mental health issues due to the lack of energy flowing upward into the higher chakras. Now this isn't to take the responsibility from those who were and are responsible for bloodshed. But you can be assured that many of the times when there were men attacking women, there may have also been a mentally and emotionally *inactivated* woman behind him rooting him on to do it.

So, how do these aspects translate into mental health disorders for many women and girls who have suffered at the hands of other women who were mentally ill? Once you have been betrayed, hated, slandered, and sabotaged by those closest to you or of "your own kind," for reasons none other than competition and jealousy due to solely operating from these lower based chakra levels, those of your own kind appear to be a threat. Her painful experiences from the same sex embedded a subconscious or unconscious default-mistrust-setting that says, "**Some of the same women I've helped were among the same ones that gathered to burn me at the stake.**"

Truth Moment: When I started independently consulting in the Intellectual/Developmental Disabilities healthcare sector, I was excited! Not because I had just begun running my own consulting company . . . NOPE! But because all of the special-needs providers I served were small, black-owned, women-owned and run companies. Yep . . . Little known fact! That meant long hours, hair tied back in ponytails, high heels off, eating lunch spread eagle on the floor with our faces buried deep in file folders, until every "t" was crossed and every "i" dotted. Because to me, this was my chance to support "my kind" in a way that would *ensure* their success and longevity. In my mind, no one would have the chance to bring them under or take away what they've worked for, but I forgot to include myself in that equation. Six years later, I decided to later relinquish my role as a consultant for good when a black female that worked in the human resources department of one of my clients, attempted to physically attack me during a staff meeting. She jumped up saying "I'm tired of you bitch, come on," and held up her dukes. She became pissed when I did not agree on the state's policy requiring consultants in my role to complete a particular set of trainings and additional workload. I decided to contact our policy department within Georgia's downtown office myself to inquire, and I found that she not only lied but tampered with policy information. Her excuse was frustration due to lack of training and policy knowledge on her end, but I knew better. You see, there had been several covert and passive-aggressive incidents toward me that occurred. I noticed that staff morale dropped immensely, and when she was present there would be snickering whenever I entered or exited a room. I'd even notice how her tone toward me came off as sharp and curt. These were all the signs that there was more happening underneath the surface than I was expecting to encounter, from the same ones I helped to establish.

When this incident occurred, I was later approached by one other female staff member who said, "***Timmésha, she and all of them just sit around and talk bad, so bad about you. She's been wanting your position from the jump because she sees how much you make. She rolls her eyes every time you walk in. She's even trying to dress better because of you. She's been telling (let's just say Jane Doe for legal purposes) that she can do your job plus more. And Jane Doe said that you're good at what you do Timmésha, but that she just can't afford you.***"

Now when this staff person shared this with me my first thoughts were:

1. It was my client who set the amount she could afford and we agreed on that. How then is it too much when your business has grown exponentially with my support?

2. Thank you for telling me these things, but if you knew all the bad things they've said about me, then they must have felt comfortable enough to say them in front of you, why?

Her response was, "I just sit back and say nothing because I wanted them to get it all out so I could come and tell you."

I came to discover that a number of the women I consulted and supported gathered together to privately ridicule my business to sabotage its foreseeable expansion and my financial stability. I even received insight that after I removed myself from my clients all together, some proceeded to take credit for the work and tools I had created.

My mama used to always say, "A dog that brings a bone will take a bone." This is a popular saying that really just means that the same person who came running to tell you some mess, more than likely will spread the mess too. Otherwise, a true friend wouldn't want to bring you news that could hurt you. She or he would take the necessary steps to report a grievance (especially in a workplace) to higher authorities, and would have told you the very first time the offense occurred without your knowledge.

I include this truth moment, because I want to point out the many ways in which mental illness shows itself in those that you've not only helped but that look just like you, and the many ways in which the concept of spell work and covens may show up in your day-to-day lives today. **A coven** is merely a group of people that gather for the same purpose, whether those purposes are of goodwill or ill-will. And harmful **spell work** may be done through incantations, i.e., the speaking of ill onto others. So in my experience, a coven of mentally ill women (aka, witches not in a healing sense) gathered together to produce spell work to attack, mock, and slander my name and ruin my business reputation. They purposely and knowingly recited harm-producing incantations by invoking negative words to poison any and all positive outcomes.

Perhaps you yourself have had the same experience I did, or others just as life-altering. If so, write the following mantra below on the page provided, recite it out loud, then burn it in a safe burning container to release the energy. ***If you're reading eBook, please use a separate sheet of paper***

"All harmful energies sent to me I send back to senders instantly. I wrap it all in immovable, unbreakable, unshakeable, and impenetrable love. May they not be able to give it away and may no one be able to take it away from them. Thank you, for your attempted attacks elevated me. And so it is forever in all eternities!"

Tear at the perforated line, then burn your written page in a safe burning container to break the harmful spells sent to you.

Timmesha Burgess

--------------------------**Perforated Line**------------------------

Activate

Just for the sake of driving the point home of women harming women long before men could, it's imperative that I point out that in today's societies, I've seen many women talk about this idea of "pussy power." But based on my research and my own evolutionary journey, I've found that a lot of these concepts are shared by women who haven't developed the emotional intelligence nor the mental health themselves to share such powerful ancient motifs.

I see many women developing seminars, doing speeches, and hosting women's conferences attempting to guide others on tapping into feminine power—and while that is great, here is what I KNOW:

- Without mental and emotional intelligence to properly wield such power, you get immature women attacking other women due to jealousy and competition.
- Women who attempt to control and belittle men with their vaginas.
- Feminine power attracts, it does not chase unless she lives in the wild and feeds on hyenas. ***Hence; those who chase men, women, status thus attempting to attach oneself to abuse and toxic relationships and marriages.***
- This power does not attack unless protecting itself and loved ones.
- You are "unequipped" to teach any knowledge about a power you yourself haven't spiritually been initiated into activating. You cannot FAKE energy and consciousness. People will be able to see your falseness before you even speak. This is the Aquarian age; therefore, hidden truths will prevail.
- Just the way we don't want to see poisonous men in positions of raw power, we don't want to see poisonous women activating this power either, not

- without having first developed the divine empathy to do so.
- The darkness (the womb) is where this feminine power lives. And unless you've traveled through the dark night of the soul journey yourself, you are "**UNEQUIPPED**" to guide anyone to it.
- Pretending to know these ancient wisdoms of feminine power will have you in a spiritual prison with the unseen forces. Perhaps it could even be actual prison in cases where this power is used to actually kill, steal, and destroy others.
- This isn't about just accessing and unleashing power, it's about earning the spiritual right to do so, and knowing what to do with it once you do.
- Men embody this energetic power too!

But let's not blame anyone for operating solely from their lower selves as *oppressors* of others, "**IF**" they haven't been previously introduced to concepts about raising their energies into their higher body and inner-mind centers. You don't know what you don't right? But when you are informed, you will be held responsible for your actions once you've been made privy to this information. So, now that you know, what actions will you take to rise? Now let's get to the final takeaway I gathered from Penny Dreadful.

4. Choosing not to carry on a pregnancy deemed the receiver and/or practitioner as heartless, callous, and non-maternal.

Do the research on the amount of abortion practitioners that were under attack over the decades. The amount of physicians that had to hurry in and out of their buildings with security just to ensure their safety is unimaginable. And why? According to Jacob Sprenger and Heinrich Kramer's witchcraft treatise, **The Malleus Maleficarum** (1487); to perform or receive such acts was perceived as devil worship and were carried out by witches (i.e., women), **"witches possessed malicious powers . . . to impede fertility"** (Blomquist, 9).

Blomquist's quote above exemplifies the idea held by *both* women and men who wrongfully accused women of malicious intent, that women who decided to terminate pregnancies were indeed possessed with malicious powers and impeded their fertility. Moreover, many women at those times birthed several children, some birthing more than thirteen or more children back-to-back—and unfortunately yet fortunately condoms weren't invented until 1855, and girls as young as ten years of age were becoming pregnant. Why? The choice wasn't on the woman or girl to decide when they wanted to be sexually intimate, but in many cases was enforced by their husbands, via sexual crimes and/or traditions such as rape, molestation, and forced marriages.

I remember the shame and guilt I felt and held in my body and mind, when I found out I was pregnant at nineteen. When I decided to terminate my pregnancy my sophomore year of undergrad, I was scared, and mad as HELL at myself. But I was ABSOLUTELY SURE of what I wanted to do and why. I was engaged at the time to a pretty good guy, he was a soldier in the United States Army and was deployed to Iraq and Kuwait for a year and a half, and I WAITED for him to return. We weren't intimate before his departure, so needless to say when he returned home from duty . . . it was on and POPPING! I got pregnant, and the rest is history. I didn't feel guilt or shame because of my decision to terminate, but because I hated the amount of exhausting energy that came along with my getting pregnant at all. I held myself to an image of "***this isn't supposed to happen to me ... not right now ... IF EVER!***" Frankly speaking, I never desired to have children of my own, especially when there were parts of me that still needed mothering and nurturing. I even remember trying to make myself feel sad that

I had chosen to terminate my pregnancy, because based on societal beliefs, I should feel bad for going through with such a thing. But I did not! I was heart, mind, and in my soul confident that I was making the BEST decision not just for myself but for that potential being. I'm now 36 years old and can confidently look back on that experience and say, "**May you be born out of the womb that is fully activated and better prepared for you, and so it shall be.**"

The thing is, many women have been taught to be ashamed of themselves for not desiring to have children. Why? Because societal or cultural norms teach that the role of a female is to get married, have babies, and "**IF** YOU CAN," get a quality education—that is, until you get married and have babies, then perhaps you can drop out and be a stay-at-home wife. Now don't get me wrong, there's nothing wrong with being a stay-at-home wife if that is what YOU choose. Hell, I've often imagined myself as a kept woman, indeed. Any woman is lying if she says she hasn't at least thought about it! But that choice should be between you and your spouse if you are both consenting adults. To others, it's considered callous to terminate a pregnancy; perhaps I am a witch who has done the work of the devil by having done so. But for the woman or girl who decides to be true to herself, it is a NONE-OF-YOUR-DAMN-BUSINESS decision!

I taught myself overtime to respond to anyone who ever asked me why I don't have children to say, "**I have birthed many seeds already, such as my love for others, ideas, dreams, innovations, laughter, and visions. However, IF I ever decide to push a human out of my vagina, you'll know it. But thank you for your concern.**" Women and girls for decades have developed guilt and shame because of their desire to terminate. Pressures by family members, religious doctrine, and others on continuing with a pregnancy even if it's not in her best interest to do so, taught her to suffer in silence. Hence, the rise and increase of anxiety and depression in her that dared to choose for herself.

It is almost hard to accept the amount of scrutiny both women and men in the field of performing terminations are consistently under because of their chosen practices, paths, and/or healing modalities. Imagine the level of anxiety and depression healthcare professionals today are still under, who are brave enough to stand with women and girls who decide otherwise. If all your life you are taught to grow up, get married, and have babies, imagine the level of mental health disorders that develop over time in those that are ostracized for wanting to make the call on whether or not motherhood is for them.

I chose to use the witch scenario from the *Penny Dreadful* series as an example of mental health disorders developed throughout the ages, because it is important to include sentinel events that began the development of repudiated parts of our psyche. Due to the fear of being categorized as the pseudo pretense of a WITCH, a term that in the seventeenth century was used to solidify the effects of opprobrium, led to the suppression of women with spiritual gifts, healing abilities, unquestionable intuition, and free will to choose rather or not they wanted to remain pregnant.

As I consider the above mentions of women and terminating pregnancies and my own personal experience with choosing to terminate, I received some ancient intuitive downloads/uploads, and channels to share with those of you on this same journey. Many may be uncomfortable with the following message; therefore, I record this as a **RED ALERT**, meaning, what follows may induce feelings of overwhelming force and shock for some. Because of this, I asked my spiritual team to guide me on sharing this part with you. As usual, I can only offer ancient wisdom to you as raw as they are downloaded, uploaded, channeled and activated within me.

Downloaded/Uploaded/ Intuitively Channeled Message

Shift your perspective on childbirth from one that is purely mundane to that which teeters on spiritual and psychological warfare. Do not look at the man or woman, but rather at the being that animates the man and woman's body. What do you see, and feel underneath their flesh costume?

For the woman considering continuing a pregnancy or termination, decipher if the being that operates inside of the man is made up of a substance that your womb should birth. Is the being within the man an enemy that wants to infiltrate your bloodline, by trying to use your womb to enter this world?

Decide if it is safe for you and everyone involved if this being is birthed into flesh. If you are impregnated by a being that operates this man's body, ask your womb if it is safe for the world if this being is birthed through you.

For the man, allow your divine inner selves to guide you in choosing if her womb has stolen your seed in hopes of infiltrating your royal bloodline; acting as a "stow away" to gain access to this world.

You have this decision-making power through termination in the event you find yourselves on the precipice of bringing forth life from the spirit world into the physical world without your purposeful planning for childbirth. In the event your womb or seed is compromised, it is considered a spiritual act of treason to your planet. A trauma that will affect you and that child's life, mind, and emotions for many lifetimes (as it has already), and the of those for generations to come.

—The All, Divine Feminine, Divine Masculine

Timmesha Burgess

According to ***Rehabilitating the Witch***, Blomquist states:

> Other scholars, like Barbara Ehrenreich and Deirdre English, point out the association between witches and medicine. They explain that men established the medical field as a male domain and argue that university trained physicians claimed control over women's bodies and destroyed the power of wise women who offered medical aid by declaring them witches. Still other scholars concentrate on the association between witchcraft and psychiatry and suggest that witches were women who were mentally ill. They contend that rudimentary medicine made it difficult to interpret bizarre behavior as anything other than supernatural. Certain feminist scholars have focused on the witch as an example of the persecution of women and of their perceived inferior status. As the witchcraft historian Carol Karlsen puts it, "the story of witchcraft was primarily the story of women," a story that showcased male fears about women and their proper place in society and demonstrated the extent to which systematic violence could be practiced against the female sex. Other feminist scholars, finally, argue that the witch plays a more complex role in feminist texts. Justyna Sempruch suggests in her recent study that the evolution of the "witch" follows the same trajectory as that of modern feminism. The witch evolved, Sempruch argues, from that (radically feminist) woman who is culturally subjugated and victimized to a superwoman of sovereign and mythical power"

Activate

According to Saint-Martin, the witch occupies a central place in the feminist mythology as a being that struggles against repressive powers. Rather than denigrate the witch character, she suggests that modem feminist texts seek to reverse previous traditions by celebrating witches as symbols of freedom and contestation. Another scholar, Marie Josephine Diamond, echoes Saint-Martin's arguments and contends that such feminist revisions of literary history have transformed the textual inscriptions of gender and paved the way for the emergence of a new genre of women writing. She suggests that "demonized madwomen " like the witch have been liberated from their enforced exile, given a new voice, and been allowed to speak and "remember history" differently. Justine Sempruch acknowledges the need to re-historicize and revitalize the witch and contends that the witch figure is a crucial metaphor for herstory, the feminist mythology constituted as an alternative to the established male-centered master narrative. And Denise Shelton believes that giving voice to the witch allows authors to uncover the complex interplay between subjectivity, the collective, and history. She contends that the witch is both a political and poetic figure who "initiates the liberating process through which the feminine can be reconfigured" (Blomquist, 14-103).

Now, almost throughout this entire book I'll be referencing texts from the thesis titled **Rehabilitating the Witch**. Why? Because I'm being guided by a ***fiery passion*** within me to *urgently* paint a clear picture of the psychological extent witch hunts had and still have in the lives, minds and bodies of almost every man, woman and child to date.

Question: Would my fiery passion classify me as a witch in previous centuries? Yes! And why? Because I exhibit behaviors that according to patriarchal beliefs about witches are, *unusual, mystical, attractive, magnetic, sensual, sexual, nonconforming, unorthodox,* and *free-willed.*

Now, let's be clear about the term *patriarchal* as it relates to this particular body of work. Although defined as *"relating to or characteristic of a system of society or government controlled by men,"* this term is not exclusively about men, but about those who abuse power wearing the flesh costume of men. It is crucial that we start to make clear distinctions of patriarchal rule by drawing a line between toxic mindsets of some men and all men. This has nothing to do with men as a whole, but sheds light on anyone (man or woman) that chooses to embody an energy that enjoys seeking to suppress others due to their own **mental illness**. Previously I drew clear differences based on my perspective, between those that exhibit mental disorder and mental illness. If you require further clarification start from the beginning of this book; however, I'll make a few more references as we continue.

For now, let us get back on track with the point and case to further draw out this clear picture of the *psychological* extent witch hunts had and still have on the mind and body of almost every man, woman and girl to date.

According to **Rehabilitating the Witch**,

> At the end of the portion of the novel that concentrates on Nadja, authorities decide that the protagonist does not behave normally, declare her mad and force her into an insane asylum. The correlation between witchlike characters and madness is not

surprising given the way society began to interpret witchcraft in the twentieth century. With the advent of psychology, psychoanalysis, and psychiatry, doctors began to question whether witches were perhaps victims of mental illnesses (Blomquist 98).

Taking the previous quote into consideration, two categorically distinct differences revealed themselves to me about whether witches (i.e., those born with natural spiritual gifts and abilities; those who didn't "behave" normally), were perhaps victimized by others with mental illness. The following questions that came up for me were:

1. Were there *mentally ill* women and men attempting to harm (**hunt/haunt**) others by misusing the power of alchemy?

2. Were there denigrated women and men naturally born with spiritual abilities being (**hunted/haunted**) by those mentally ill?

I'll end this chapter with a YouTube video by Sadhguru, that was guided to me to watch in 2019. I say guided because on this journey you learn fairly quickly that the teacher appears when the student is ready. Although I was not specifically searching for anything Sadhguru or the topic of witches at all, this video through cosmic alignment and divine intervention found its way to me. When I saw the title, I knew I was being compelled to view it, as the title alone fit the description of a speech I was preparing myself to conduct, titled **"The Divine Feminine Reborn**." A speech that was heard in six different continents and developed by new-thought leaders from India, the United States and beyond. Sadhguru's video was titled, "**Can a woman become a Goddess (the world needs witches)**", from the Devi Fire of the Feminine series. In the video he says,

My great grandma. People used to say she's a devil of a woman . . .They called her devil of a woman not because she ever did any harm to anybody, but she had a laugh. If she laughed the entire street shook... She lived to be 113 years of age... When she was 68yrs years of age after her husband died, she went out and built a small temple for herself. She did not install a God, she installed herself in the temple. She did her own type of worship, her own type of everything. She could tell you anything, when she's there sitting in the temple, she can just tell you about anything in the world. You know the history of Europe where spiritual process was so widespread, and how systematically it was so uprooted and thrown out when they wanted to establish an organized religion. So all those millions of witches who were burned, are just those women who exhibited certain qualities that did not fit into the logical logic of that society. My great grandmother would for sure have been burned as a witch. In India they wouldn't burn, but they were afraid of her laughter . . . She's definitely a witch! So we need witches. We need witches in the world, we need women who are more capable than their logic. We need men who are also like that, we need human beings who are capable of perceiving, understanding, experiencing life beyond the horrible limitations of logic.

I must say that I only partly agree with Sadhguru that the world needs witches, my only addition to this wise quote is quite the agreeable contrary. In my thorough opinion, based on my own personal life's journeys, research, and internally activated ancient wisdom, I say that the world needs mentally balanced and emotionally intelligent witches. Those men and women who are naturally born with the spiritual, empathic, and psychic abilities of clairvoyance, intuitive insights, and healing capabilities; to evolve a world built on pain, to one that thrives in its own born-with-it power.

Timmesha Burgess

CHAPTER 2: MENTAL DISORDERS & SEXUAL TRAUMA

Witch hunts as previously mentioned, weren't just the killing of women who chose to operate completely from their lower bodies (although there were definitely MANY that did); but attacks by those who wanted her beauty, talents, skills, wisdom, intellect, spiritual abilities, and womb energy a.k.a. *pussy power*. What may have looked like witches attacking *certain* men, were in many cases women trying to protect themselves and their loved ones from **rape, molestation, kidnapping, forced relationships or marriages**, and other exploitive rituals wrapped in what some call "religious" or "cultural" *traditions* and law.

As it relates to heinous acts being masked under the auspices of religious and cultural traditions, and even under the protection of "the law." Let's for a moment consider two distinct story lines from past to present day as it relates to this chapter on *mental disorders and sexual trauma*. First, the true story of **Jezebel (past),** and the second being today's organization called the **Istanbul Convention (present day)**; so, let's begin with Jezebel.

JEZEBEL SPEAKS

I include the story of Jezebel because even as a teenager, during my days as a devout Christian (as many in Western societies were raised to be or else to hell you go. Which we know or will know soon, is exactly where we want to go or already are), I always had a weird sort of uneasy feeling in my stomach when Jezebel was preached about in church. I would cringe when anyone would spew the name Jezebel out of their mouths, not because of her name, but because something within me deeply knew there was more to the story. And that whoever she was, she had been unfairly judged and perpetually misunderstood.

Now, throughout this book you know that I've been including "ah-ha" and truth moments that opened up for me, even in the process of writing this book. Well here's another one for you. As I'm writing this work I receive tons of downloads, and uploads from my ancient self, ancestors, and my personal spiritual team. Information that I am compelled to include in this book, or else I can't sleep or rest until I do. The information will play over and over in my stomach, mind, and heart until I jot it down and until I actually get it in this book.

So, one evening I was in meditation at my altar in my bedroom, and the song **Jezebel** by singer/songwriter **Sade** kept playing on repeat in my head. All I could do was continue singing the beginning words of "**Jezebeeeel, do you really want to know she says . . . Jezebel, do you really want to know she saaaaays.**" Again, I suggest pausing at this point of the book and pulling up the song for yourself before continuing to read. Anyway, this is really the only line of the song that played over and over inside my mind, so much so that I had to grab my phone to listen to it and read along with the lyrics. After I listened and cried, I called my mom to discuss what came to me during my meditation. My mom even cried and shared what was downloaded within her from her ancient self. We both laughed and cried from the understanding, innerstanding, and overstanding that the spirit of Jezebel wanted her justice, and her true story to be told! That night, with my candles lit and my heart wide open, I said out loud, "**Yes, Jezebel I really want to know.**" The very next day, YouTube suggested a movie for me to watch, and I bet you can guess the title of the film, that's right, but it was spelled **Jessabelle**. Jessabelle is an American supernatural horror film directed by Kevin Greutert and written by Ben Garant. The film stars Sarah Snook, Mark Webber, Joelle Carter, David Andrews,

Amber Stevens, and Ana de la Reguera, and was released by Lionsgate on November 7, 2014.

I planned my day so that I could relax and think of nothing else but to sit and enjoy this movie, and enjoy it I did! The movie was about a young white woman who grew up in Louisiana, under the care of two well established land and slave owners. Turns out that Jessabelle wasn't really the daughter of her parents, but was adopted, and the real Jessabelle was murdered at birth. Why? Because the mother slept with a local black man, got pregnant, and gave birth to a mixed baby. When the husband saw this, he killed the baby viciously. He then went out and adopted the white child and renamed her Jessabelle. So, the spirit of the real Jessabelle, who happened to be a beautiful black female, wanted her life back!

Now although movie writers are creative and produce movies based on the best way to entertain audiences, what I got from it was much more profound than a normal day-to-day person just sitting down to enjoy a good flick. What came to me was, "**Wow, look at how we accept one and reject the other, look at who we accept what is considered the light (white), and reject the dark (black). Not just in race and culture throughout time, but as it relates to our inner worlds and spiritual senses.**" This movie opened up Pandora's box in a way, and revealed to me that what we attempt to hide, disguise, suppress, and vilify into the darkness of culture, traditions, religion, and beliefs always . . . always come back up to not only haunt us but also to take their rightful place. In the case of this written work, haunting of the mind is a mental disorder brought on by the continuous split between that which is considered dark and that which is called light.

Until you decide to watch the movie yourself, let's do a quick check in. Here is an assignment to gauge where you are right

Activate

now as it relates to your inner, under, and overstanding of the dark and light.

    Below is a photo of the movie cover. Study the front cover, and transcribe in the space provided what is activated within you as you stare at the dark and light female images. As you stare at the image, write all that is channeled, uploaded, and downloaded through you. As you do, you will be personally activating your ancient and suppressed power. By simply doing this practice, your hidden self will begin to come out of hiding, and you will begin the process of understanding, innerstanding, and overstanding the relationship between your own dark and light selves. By doing this practice, you are beginning the activation of your suppressed superpower. If you have a personal journal, use it to continue writing if you require more pages. Refer to this portion of **Activate** as often as you need, to solidify your newly activated wisdom. **If you're reading eBook, please use a separate sheet of paper**

DARK & LIGHT PRACTICE AND THE ACTIVATION OF JEZEBEL'S TRUTH

Image cropped from https://www.rottentomatoes.com/m/jessabelle

Timmesha Burgess

According to Worldhistory.org,

> For more than two thousand years, Jezebel has been saddled with a reputation as the bad girl of the Bible, the wickedest of women. This ancient queen has been denounced as a murderer, prostitute, and enemy of God, and her name has been adopted for lingerie lines and World War II missiles alike. But just how depraved was Jezebel? In recent years, scholars have tried to reclaim the shadowy female figures whose tales are often only partially told in the Bible. Although she has been associated with seduction, depravity, and harlotry for centuries, a more accurate understanding of Jezebel emerges as one considers the possibility she was simply a woman who refused to submit to the religious beliefs and practices of her husband and his culture. The recent scholarship, which has led to a better understanding of the civilization of Phoenicia, the role of women, and the struggle of the adherents of the Hebrew god Yahweh for dominance over the older faith of the Canaanites, suggests a different, and more favorable, picture of Jezebel than the traditional understanding of her. The scholarly trend now is to consider the likely possibility she was a woman ahead of her time married into a culture whose religious class saw her as a formidable threat.

Jezebel's untold or (mis)told story as it relates to this chapter on mental disorder and sexual trauma, and as it relates to the above quoted text, is one of many kinds. So far, we've dissected the heinous acts of the witch hunts that sought to smite any and every woman from the planet that displayed particular abilities and just so happened to also be beautiful. This also happened during the Crusades. To these perspectives of Jezebel as a woman with strong opinions, who happened to be beautiful and powerful enough to shatter false concepts of "Only our God and nothing else" during the time of a religious take-over, sheds light on the toxic patriarchal conception of Jezebel. The false perception painted of Jezebel taught women and girls (and men) all over the world one thing, and one thing only: *if she's beautiful, strong, intelligent, and could wield a sword to chop the head of anyone that attempts to kill, steal, and destroy her based on their own selfish intent, then she's an evil thing sent from devil and the pits of hell.*

What I learned through my meditation, and channeling of Sade's song, and by watching the film was in a nutshell heart-wrenching yet liberating as I uncovered Jezebel's truth.

- **Was she a woman who possessed intuitive gifts and dressed well?**

    Yes! She was born into a royal bloodline. Jezebel was a princess already before marrying into a monarchy. Therefore, it was normal for her to wear makeup, jewelry, and dress a certain way due to her prestige. This was a norm for any man or woman of certain noble standard, as it has always been. There was never any clear information on whether or not Jezebel even wanted to be married off, but theologians who took the time to study her lineage found that her marriage was the decision of a political treaty between their kingdoms and the two families.

- **Did she arouse men near and far for reasons known and unknown?**

    Sure! But texts only convey that she purposely did so and not that she was naturally magnetic due to her beauty and being of noble blood. Texts NEVER made mention that Jezebel was merely made a victim of her environment, due to toxic masculinity that wanted to control and put a lid on her mind, body, power, and forward-thinking.

- **Did Jezebel impose godless beliefs on people who were taught to believe only in one God?**

    Why not? Especially if that one God told people to kill, rape, and steal from others if they didn't comply with whatever was imposed upon them! Jezebel was an anomaly in a world where toxic masculinity was the beginning and end-all of rule. Her presence was proof that there was knowledge that lay outside the boundaries of religiosity. Her power to question that which was enforced upon others was a threat to their plan to usurp sovereignty, block the ability to think for self, and sever the chords that connected each individual to the God/Goddess within.

Jezebel was the mirror to the sexual desires of those who lacked emotional intelligence and mental health, not because she tried to be, but because they had no control over themselves when she was present. Jezebel's story draws a parallel between mental disorder and sexual trauma as it relates to the degradation and suppression of natural sensual prowess and power. Because if they couldn't control it, buy it, sell it, or steal it away themselves, they would lie and say she gave it away.

> **Activated/Channeled/Downloaded/Uploaded Message**
>
> If there are any among you who have been called Jezebels due to your desire for sexual pleasure; the sexual exploitation of your power is all your own doing and desire, and has NOTHING to do with the spirit of Jezebel, NO! If any among you truly possesses the "**Jezebel spirit,**" as your religious doctrine likes to call it, then she would be lightyears from promiscuity. She would have no need to pimp herself for wealth, or sell her power for gain, why? Because such as in the *true* story of Jezebel, she that is among you would already be born DNA-coded with her own riches, and glory—in more ways than one.
>
> — Jezebel, The Ancient Ones

THE ISTANBUL CONVENTION

This is a human rights treaty of the Council of Europe that protect and prevent violence against women and girls. According to reports from BBC, CNN, and others, women poured into the streets in 2021 to protest against Turkey removing themselves from the treaty. A bbc.com report states, "**Opponents of the convention have complained it encourages divorce and undermines traditional family values**" (yalcinalp BBC.com).

Although not difficult to ascertain, it is clear that even today there are many that choose to call crimes against women traditional family values, which really translates as, "*I should be able to beat, rape, abuse, kill, and force the continuance of an abusive marriage upon any woman I wish to at any time with complete impunity from any legal obligations, because it's within my traditional family values to do so.*" Why do I include this tidbit of information in this chapter of mental disorder and sexual trauma? Because a number of women in countries such as Turkey who have undergone sexual trauma through forced

Activate

marriages and/or relationships, are suffering not just from physical but also psychological abuse, and sexual subjugation.

To paint a full picture of the psychological effects of sexual trauma, consider the chart below for example. Let's begin to explore numbers one through three:

1. Fear and anxiety regarding issues of survival.

2. Fear and anxiety regarding issues of intimacy and relationships, usually caused by previous violation of this space.

3. Frustration, powerlessness, and stagnation which leads to anger.

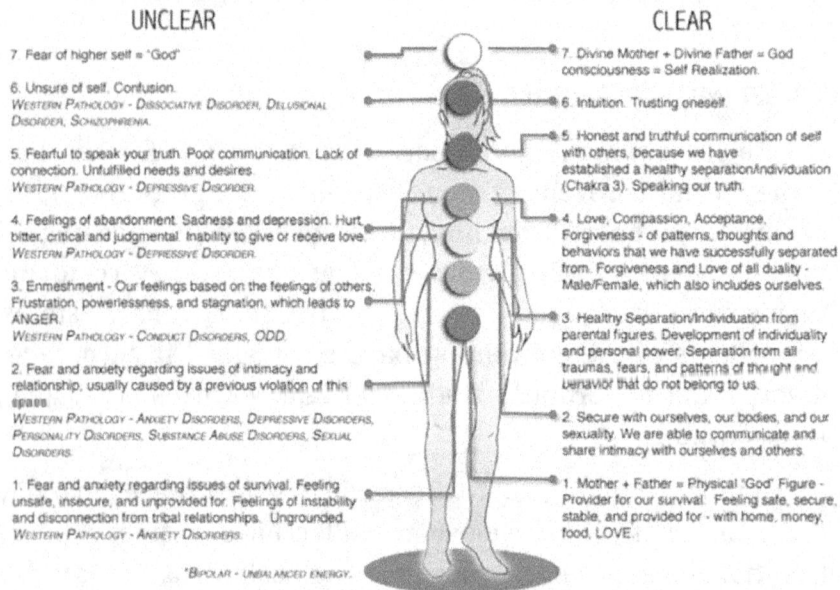

Photo taken from Psychodynamic and Spiritual Awakening Counseling (psychodynamicawakening.com)

Take notice of the three lowest chakra centers in the diagram above: the root chakra (red), sacral chakra (orange), and solar chakra (yellow). The lower-level chakras house what we understand to be our sensual and sexual power in the areas of our vaginas and our wombs. When these chakra centers are misused, abused, and usurped through sexual trauma, the experiencer develops what we call mental disorder. How? Because the brunt of sexual trauma is directed at these centers of the body, and suppresses the power of these lower chakra centers within them. This causes energy to remain stuck and/or stolen from within these centers of the energetic bodies of the experiencer. In this case, energy is unable to fully rise up for activation throughout the rest of the body, causing continued mental disorder (instability) due to the lack of energy flowing upward into the higher mind and bodies. In a nutshell, all of her power remains trapped in her lower body, unable to rise up into her mind. Therefore, the mental imbalance is due to all of her power remaining trapped below or stolen away through sexual trauma.

As I journeyed through the darkness of my own mind and into what lies beneath a typical diagnosis incurred from painful experiences, I uncovered deep revelations about why and how anxiety and depression showed up for me and for many women who have survived sexual trauma and/or are currently in the midst of it. I was led to ask and **answer** three (3) important questions that would ultimately activate the powers I and so many have held in our mind and body for several generations and even several lifetimes.

1. **Can suicidal thoughts, anxiety, and depression actually be the symptoms or side effects of deeply suppressed energy, wanting to be acknowledged and set free?**
2. **What makes our feminine power so valuable that throughout history, schemes have been created to hide it, usurp it, sell it, buy it, and seek to control it?**
3. **Is *fear* of feminine power an *undiagnosed* mental disorder or mental illness?**

Activate

According to a research article published in the **Harvard T.H. Chan School of Public Health on sexual assault**, relating to harassment linked with long-term health problems in women:

> Women in mid-life who are survivors of sexual assault and harassment can experience long-term physical and mental health problems including high blood pressure, anxiety, depression, and insomnia, according to a new study. Co-authored by Karestan Koenen, professor of psychiatric epidemiology at Harvard T.H. Chan School of Public Health and colleagues from the University of Pittsburgh, the study looked at 304 women between the ages of 40 and 60. In that group, 19% reported experiencing sexual harassment, 22% reported experiencing sexual assault, and 10% reported both. Sexual assault survivors were three times more likely to experience depression and twice as likely to have more anxiety than women who hadn't been sexually assaulted (Koenen).

According to article, "Sexual Abuse and Lifetime Diagnosis of Psychiatric Disorders: Systematic Review and Meta-analysis published in NCBI" (U.S. National Library of Medicine National Institutes of Health);

> Sexual abuse is associated with multiple psychiatric disorders, including lifetime diagnosis of anxiety disorders, depression, eating disorders, PTSD, sleep disorders, and attempted suicide. Improved recognition of the link between a history of sexual abuse and mental health disorders may increase the identification of abuse survivors and lead to better treatment and

outcomes (Chen, Murad, Paras, Colbenson, Sattler, Goranson, Elamin, Seime, Shinozaki, Prokop & Zirakzadeh).

In ***Rehabilitating the Witch***, Blomquist states the following:

> "Witches" are victims of the sabbat. They do not seek the Devil to satiate their sexual desires and do not try to use their sexuality to control male interests. In fact, the twentieth century authors suggest the opposite; their witches are prey to male sexual fantasies. First, in Vassalli and Hebert's novels, both Antonia and soeur Julie are physically abused and dehumanized while male inquisitors search their bodies for their stigma diabolis (Blomquist 46).

The stigma diabolis translates as the mark of the devil that abusers called themselves looking for on each woman or girl they violated. In ***Rehabilitating the Witch*** it reads as follows:

> In *La Chimera* and *Les Enfants du sabbat*, Vassalli and Hebert's witch characters must undergo torturous examinations. Their literary witches are thoroughly examined in a process that is cruel, long, and inhumane. Because they know that the process is lengthy and painful, those who examine soeur Julie decide to tie her to the bed while she is still asleep before they begin their inspection. Hebert paints a disturbing portrait of soeur Julie during the process; she writes that the witch protagonist is bound, shaven, and so brutally searched that she loses the ability to speak . . . Instead of crying out and communicating, the witch protagonist can only

spit to express her disgust as her persecutors pierce her body with needles for hours upon end . . . . In *La Chimera*, Vassalli's likens Antonia's inspection to a rape scene. We learn that Taddeo conducts a minute inspection of Antonia's naked body and is so thorough that he looks under Antonia's tongue and in all of the most intimate parts of her body . . . Taddeo searches Antonia's body as if he were making love to her. He begins with her mouth, opens her legs, and then penetrates all of her orifices. And it is obvious that he enjoys the process- Vassalli writes that Taddeo won the "privilege" by tossing for it with his son . . . Male inquisitors violate and explore Antonia's and soeur Julie's naked bodies as they search for proof of their associations with the Devil. The searches, as Vassalli points out with his description, are a form of sexual assault. The witches are threatened by the overwhelming force and violence of their perpetrators. They are the tied down, gagged, and naked subjects of their male inquisitors' desire for power and sexual gratification . . . . Even these inhumane inspections seem minimal when we compare them to the extreme violation of the witches' bodies that occurs during the various rape scenes in the twentieth-century texts. In three of the four novels, the witches are brutally and violently raped. In *Les Enfants du sabbat*, Hebert's witch is forced to have sex with the Devil at the sabbat, but she is also raped continuously by her father . . . Alone in the woods, soeur Julie's father violates her again and again. She cries out, but her father ignores her pleas. In *La Chimera*, Antonia is raped and tortured simultaneously while she is in prison. Bernando and his father force her to have sex with them with a torture device in her mouth so that she cannot scream. Vassalli writes that the two "possessed her again and again" because they could not stand the thought of her "cunt" having it off with devils (Blomquist 48-50).

Considering the above quoted texts, particularly "because they could not stand the thought of her 'cunt' having it off with the devils," one could already gather together the breadcrumbs of when and where normalizing sexual abuse and other sexual crimes began to sprout during the witch hunts. And how overtime these crimes began to be masked underneath what are called "traditions." Traditions that today continue to breed generations of mental disorders in those victimized, and mental illness in those that enforce these acts.

As I write this, I am receiving and unlocking ancient wisdoms within me; therefore, I am guided to share with you this downloaded/uploaded/activated channeled message. As usual, I can only give it to you the way it's given to me so here goes.

Downloaded/Uploaded/Intuitively Channeled Message

One of the quotes shared previously reads "the two possessed her again and again" because they could not stand the thought of her 'cunt' having it off with devils." According to their beliefs, ***possessing*** her body would be considered an act of the devil. Is this not so? By ***possession*** this would mean that they were the only devils present to ***possess*** her. You tell her that she is having sex with the devil, and you are CORRECT! Because you were the only devils she knew. You taught her to neglect the devil in herself, but to submit to the devil in you. You taught her that the devil within her was wicked and evil, so that you could force her to *comply* with the devil within you.

> This wordplay on her emotions and her mind caused disorder and confusion in her; thus, training her like a slave to succumb not to her own supposed wickedness, but to yours, how clever!
>
> Disorder in her mind and body aren't only due to the traumas themselves, but due to the suppression of her power as a result of the trauma. With trauma as the cause, and the suppression of her feminine power equaling the effect. Suppression by them due to their mental illness, and suppression by her due to her fear of herself thus causing her inner power to be disordered. Her abused, misused, and confused feminine energy is now showing up as anxiety and depression.
>
> However, she now embarks on a new journey where *you no longer possess her, because she has learned to possess herself.*
>
> She will from now until forever know that anxiety and depression are her proof, that what she suppresses is more than pain, but power.
>
> **—The Ancestors, The All, The Ancient Ones**

Anxiety and depression shows up strongly and will increase over time for those who have not been taught how to properly activate their own feminine power, contrary to the experience of sexual trauma, child-bearing, or just sitting on it through the practice of "waiting for marriage." Why? Because there is stagnant energy with nothing to do and nowhere to go other than on someone else, or being misused and abused by those who have claimed her for keeps. Outside of just being plain ole predators, this knowledge of stored energy may also be the reason why pedophiles believe she or he is ripe for the picking. Hence the heinous acts of rape, molestation, and in some cultures child marriage, and female genitalia mutilation (FGM).

Early 2021, I was led to write an article titled, **"The Power of Celibacy and Abstinence They Never Wanted You to Know."** It explored the power of sensual and sexual energy by coloring outside the lines of traditional ideologies on what else sexual energy could be activated for. In it, I mentioned that girls begin to feel the onset of their feminine energy as young as ten years old, depending on when she approaches her cycle. She's at an age when this power begins to bubble underneath the surface, but there is no one around to teach her exactly what this power is. Instead of teaching her ways in which she can activate this energy (outside of reaching an age to maturely participate in sex), and if her seed hasn't already been plucked from her unwillingly through sexual abuse—then she is taught to *vilify* it, *shun* it, *hide* it, and even put on a "promise" ring that makes her vow to never uncover it until she's married. This notion does one thing only, "**teach her that the only power her body is worth, is if a man finds value in it first!**" And we wonder why she's angry, contemplates suicide, is anxious, depressed, confused about herself and life, and feels powerless!

After writing that article and sharing it publicly with the world, I was inspired to redefine the meaning of pussy power to one that is spelled as, "**Pŏosē Power,**" and is defined as **the ability to activate womb energy to build, heal, and fortify. Why? Because she can awaken and arouse the spirit of her yoni for more than just penetration.**

So, one evening, I was in a private meditation at home on a full moon night, and I decided to light a black candle to help dissolve/remove the attachments to people, places, and things that I found myself frequently accepting. As I started to do the work to open myself up to release attached energies from my mind and body, I was intuitively led to lay all the way down on the floor, spread my legs into a birthing position facing west, and push! Out of nowhere I just started pushing. I mean I pushed like I was giving birth to the biggest invisible baby anyone had ever birthed. I cried, and I pushed, and I cried, and I pushed. I did this for so long that I started to sweat. About two days later,

I was sitting on my toilet when all of a sudden a clear/mucus-like substance flowed out of me. I thought to myself for a quick minute that I needed to see a doctor, but also that I had not long before seen a physician for a routine check-up that included pap smear and blood work. Surely this couldn't be something related to a health concern or the doctor would have picked it up then; nor did it feel necessary for me to think something just happened to lay dormant and show up all of sudden. I calmed my mind and asked out loud, "*What the hell is this?!*"

A couple of weeks later, I was out and about and noticed a bookstore I had not seen before. I decided to stop and roam around inside, when suddenly I was led to pick up a book titled, **Sacred Woman:** *A Guide to Healing The Feminine Body, Mind, and Spirit* by *Queen Afua*. The male store owner out of the blue asked, "*Have you heard about that book? I hear a lot of sistas talking about it, so I was wondering what you thought if you have*." I intuitively knew that I was being guided to purchase this book because as I read the back cover, I was taken aback that it encompassed deep insight into the very nature of the experience I had weeks prior. At this point on my journey through the darkness of my mind and body, I was no stranger to divine alignments happening like this regularly. I had no doubt that by the amount of synchronicities, sleep/dream experiences, and meditation breakthroughs I was receiving, that I was being divinely guided to the right people, places, and things at the most exquisite times. I purchased the book, and within a few days I received clear insight that my experience with the mucus flowing out of me was the direct effect of my birthing meditation. It was a clear indication of the removal of stuck, stagnant, and suppressed energy that I held in my womb from past relationships, molestation, and day-to-day life pains.

In my inner darkness, I realized that I had hidden deep within me all of the sexual traumas not just from childhood molestation by a female babysitter, but also by the usurping of my sensual and sexual power from toxic male counterparts that I called romantic relationships. My physical and emotional bodies were stiffened due to the misuse and mistreatment of my feminine power. Therefore, energetic debris lying dormant was finally being released from my unconscious grasp. I intuitively knew that all the years I allowed her to be usurped was a thing of the past, but a series of painful lessons that led to her ultimate freedom.

> Take a look at all your womb experiences as lessons. Trauma by trauma, your womb will begin to release the baggage that adds up to mental, spiritual, and physical disease ... Through seven days of fasting and prayer and spiritual baths, release the emotional venom out of your womb, your Body Temple" (Afua, 59).

The rising of anxiety and depression for the woman and girl who somehow survived sexual trauma means that it is PAST time to teach her HOW TO channel her power for herself first, rather than teaching her to wait for someone else to do it on her behalf or worse, wait for someone to take or buy it from her. If we continue to avoid the inner **dark-work** necessary to *raise* suppressed energy upward into our minds and bodies, then we will continue to perpetuate generational-psychological curses (mental health disorders that cycle through generations) on girls that become women who won't understand themselves or their power outside of being claimed by a partner, and/or through sexual exploitation. There will continue to be a generation of women, girls, boys, and men; who through the misuse and abuse of sexual power are taught that love is painful and pain is love.

> ### Downloaded/Uploaded/Activated Channeled Message
>
> This is the idea of how "they," meaning those that seek to steal your power, were able to do so through treacherous acts such as these. They were able to dethrone you, steal and occupy your throne while you were sleeping—your throne being your body. They were able to sit on your throne, meaning occupy your body, having their way with it while you "the you within" slept. The idea was to overthrow the kingdom of *you*. Now that you are awake, it is time for you to reclaim your throne and your kingdom. To regain your power after sexual trauma you must re-awaken your sleeping giant. Re-awaken your dark Goddess so that you can place her (i.e., your stolen and/or suppressed superpower) back on its throne and regain its crown.
>
> ## —The Divine Feminine

Now let's for a moment imagine that we are girls no older than twelve years of age and/or women living in a small town made up of the majority of men during a time between the 16th and 18th century. Not just any kind of men, but those who held and abused their high-level positions in the church and courts of law, organizations that were the end and begin-all of rulership. Now imagine being forced to marry due to having no skill to earn on your own (possibly to someone abusive in every way imaginable), being raped, and becoming pregnant without the protection of women's rights. Your only options are to have the baby or find someone to help you terminate the pregnancy.

Imagine **being a young girl or woman** (*even if you are male reading this portion*) **living between the 15th and 18th century with no money, no rights, young, afraid, and pregnant due to rape or a forced marriage. On the pages below, write a short letter to your ancient self, advising on what she (YOU) should do to not only survive, but also to thrive. DON'T write what you think sounds appropriate or politically correct. Be completely honest**

in your advice even if it seems unorthodox, weird, dark, and taboo. Help set her (yourself) free! **If you're reading eBook, please use a separate sheet of paper**

_____
_____
_____
_____
_____
_____
_____
_____
_____
_____
_____
_____
_____
_____
_____

As I delve deeper into this chapter, I must say I feel a deep reservoir of sentiment, bitterness, and sweetness. That even as this book is being written through me, I too am being taken back down memory lane to past lives I once loved and hated. Why? Because I deeply sense the nostalgia of those in my past lives that both loved me for who and what I was and am, but hated me for the same reasons. And at the juncture within this written work, I'm being reminded of a movie I was spiritually guided to watch in 2020 on Netflix (yes Netflix again—well, creatives are everywhere telling our/your stories), called **Bulbbul**. If you haven't seen it, you'll want to watch it after reading this chapter; In fact, I would suggest you pause and go watch, listen to, and read every reference I share in this book after each point in which I reference them. If you're on this journey to uncovering your superpower, you will be compelled to without me even suggesting it. Anyway, in the movie there's a young girl who was married off at the age of about five to a man clearly in his fifties. She grew to become a beautiful woman, yet she was meek, docile, and subservient as she was raised and trained to be. One night, her husband who was once obsessed with her, accused her of cheating, not by his own decree, but because the wife of his mentally ill brother planted the lie in his head due to her jealousy of the woman's natural beauty and grace. The woman that was married off to the mentally ill brother instead of the rich one, hated that both brothers loved the main character and not her. As I mentioned in chapter one, more than not, if there was a fucked up man attacking a woman, nine times out of ten, there was a mentally ill woman behind him rooting him on to do it. Anyway, he then beat her until her feet turned inward. She lay in bed motionless, paralyzed, and torn into pieces from the inside out. To make matters worse, the brother of her husband who was mentally ill, raped her in her immovable state. She cried and screamed for help, but no one came. He raped her so brutally that she fell into a deep coma. But in her coma is where the magic took place, ultimately setting her free and saving her life. While she was in her sleep state (i.e., the inner darkness) she met herself—except this her that she met was bold, powerful, charming, and unapologetic. She offered to trade places with the bruised, beaten, and broken girl, and the girl agreed. When she awoke from her coma, she was never the same. To make a long story short, she unleashed a part of herself that she suppressed within since childhood. And the woman, aka the witch, that emerged was unstoppable; In fact, *The Indian Express*, an online media company writes a review of the film saying:

Timmesha Burgess

> A beautiful woman is dangerous. If she smiles to herself, or is self-contained, or has the temerity to express her inner thoughts which are connected solely to her being, or isn't automatically or permanently subservient to the men she is surrounded by, she is doubly dangerous (indianexpress.com).

If you have survived any of the following or other sexual traumas, then you may be experiencing *extreme* levels of anxiety and depression. If this is the case for you, then think of anxiety and depression as the symptoms, side effects, and signs of something much more powerful bubbling *underneath* the surface of your trauma.

1. Rape/Molestation
2. FGM (Female Genitalia Mutilation)
3. Child Marriage
4. Sex-Trafficking
5. Prostitution

Do you realize that all five (5) factors mentioned involve **the stealing and suppression** of reproductive power? Why do you think this is? Well, one theory of the ***Activate*** philosophies I share here would suggest that oppressors want to *use, capitalize, control, harness,* and *produce* from your feminine power, but do not want you to. To better explain, I've allowed the "**all knowing**" to channel through me to communicate this concept with you more deeply. As usual, I can only share this insight with you in the manner in which it is given to and through me from my invisible guides and ancient self, so here goes...

Downloaded/Uploaded/Intuitively Channeled Message

There are many that know the power of your womb but you do not. Your womb is more than just a vessel to reproduce human life; it is also a conduit to birth wisdom, healing, and wellbeing in more ways than you can understand in this lifetime. Which is why they want to usurp and capitalize from it, but do not want you to. Your experience with sexual trauma taught you that your womb power was nothing more than something to be taken, bought, and sold. But have you ever asked yourself why? How can something they taught you was nothing more than an object of sexual encounter be so highly sought after if you were so worthless? They (the ill ones) are aware that your ability to feel into your body is how you activate your power, so they insist on cutting away at your outer mechanisms in hopes that this will cut you off from your power. Why? It truly is not just because they fear you, but because they **envy you**. They envy your power to birth a new-age—a new age that makes their existence *obsolete*. You have developed disorder in your mind and in your body because you are not *fully* activating your own power, instead your power has been misused, abused, suppressed and/or hidden away in you until someone comes along to buy it or steal it. It is being bought by way of a marriage or relationship you may or may not have been ready for, and stolen through sexual exploitation. Sexual trauma has taught you how to hide in the dark from those trying to hurt you. Many of you who have experienced some sort of sexual trauma, more than likely experienced it from someone you and your family knew well! You taught yourself how to hide because you knew her/his pedophile lover, family or friend was watching you. To regain your mental and emotional stability, it is now time for you to play the game of hide and seek with yourself. You've hidden it in the darkness of you or it has been hidden in the darkness from you. So go and seek in the dark, do the inner dark work so that you may access, unleash, and raise your power up for full activation. Seek and ye shall find.

— The Ancient Ones, The Ancestors, The All

Timmesha Burgess

    The following picture is a drawing I did after one of my many meditations, where I would focus on releasing any and all stuck energy from my own sexual trauma of molestation. With tears in my eyes, disgust in my gut, and anger in my heart, I saw this image in my mind's eye and was immediately led to draw it as best I could. It was what my shadow self-showed me while I was focusing on healing my womb, my root chakra where sexual trauma is stored. Little did I know that not only would I be working to heal the wound of sexual trauma, but simultaneously after doing this bit of inner work, that I was also gaining access to "the" alchemical process *that turns pain into power.* Allow it to act as a lens into your own inner body, showing you where your feminine power lay stuck, trapped, and hidden as a result of sexual exploitation.

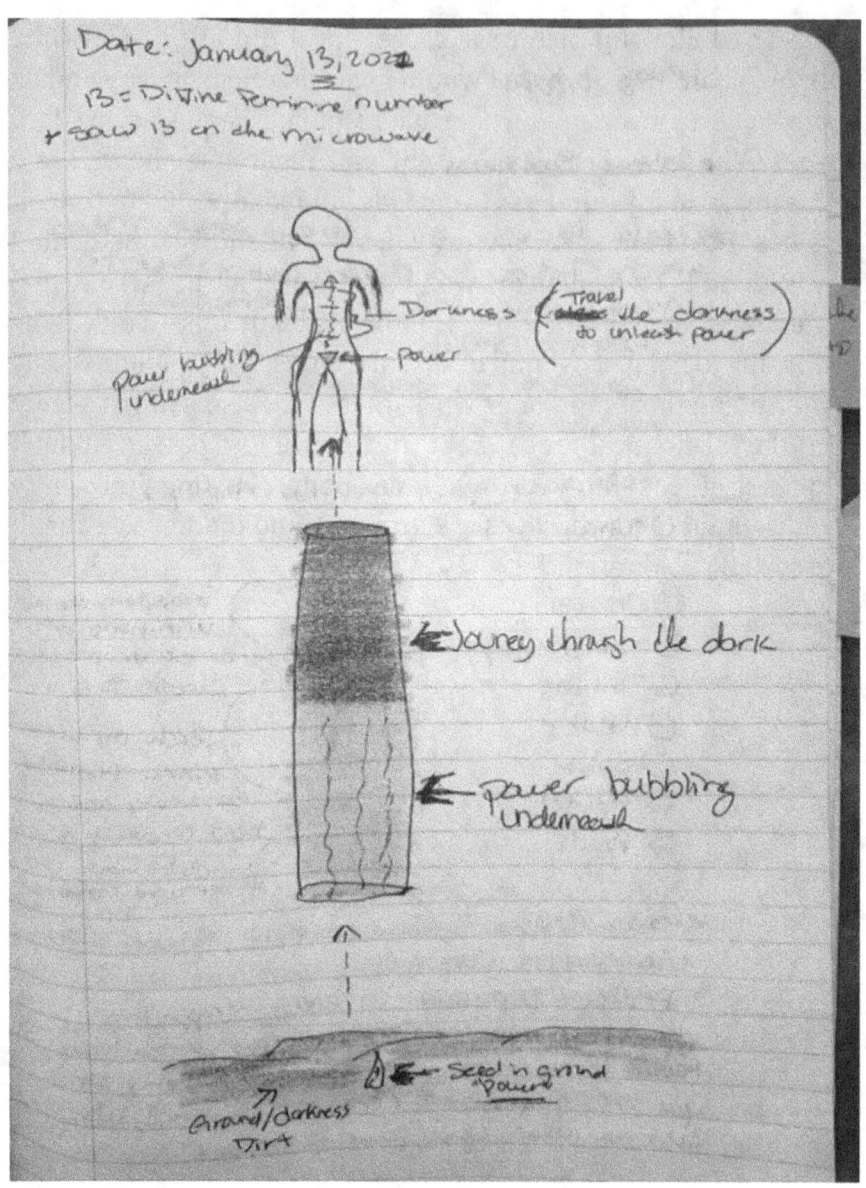

Vision sketch of trapped power by Timmésha Burgess

In the photo you notice that the yellow-colored portion represents the suppressed power within the body, and the dark portion above it represents the darkness (*dark night of the soul journey, i.e., darkness through the mind and body*) that must be navigated to access and activate your power. I mention access to this power because the journey through the dark is the path to get *to* this power; however, to *activate* the power once accessed is another. Not to worry, we'll circle back on the process of truly activating your newly accessed power in the coming chapters, so pay close attention as we continue.

My sketch shows yellow power bubbling underneath the surface—this power shows up as **anxiety** and the darkness above it reflects **depression** (the act of pressing down or in). Notice the ground in the image where it reads "***seed in the ground***." Through sexual trauma, forced marriages, or unfulfilling relationships the power that this seed releases is stolen repeatedly, never being able to reach its full potential due to the misuse of sexual energy. I also find it crucial to point out the date this image came to me which was January 13, 2021. In-addition, I noticed the number 13 flashing across my microwave the moment I was drawing this image. I intuitively knew that what I saw in my mind's eye was a revelation into the unseen world of signs and symbols meant to guide me on the course of accessing my hidden power and ancient wisdom.

According to The Shamnic Astrology Mystery School,

> Some say, like the ancient Celtic and Norse peoples, 13 is a LUCKY number, and on Friday the 13th they took time to celebrate the Goddess because Friday is named after Freya the Norse name for Venus and 13 is her sacred number. So Friday the 13th was the perfect day to make love or do other ceremonies in honor of the Goddess. Plus, there are 5 Venus cycles that occur every 8 years and in that 8 years Venus goes around the Sun 13 times. This links to the Fibonacci Sequence because 8 plus 5 equals 13. For many 13 represents the return of the Divine

Feminine including the mysteries connected with Mary Magdalene, Mother Mary, Shekinah and Sophia representing the natural rhythms and cycles coming into sacred balance. 13 is also thought to be the essence of the empowered and embodied Christed Feminine. Some say 13 is a number that transcends matter and is coded with the frequencies of Ascension, Oneness, and Unity that transforms all things. Since 13 is a prime number it is only divisible by itself representing purity—as 13 then is incorruptible and exists within its own integrity. Turtle NumbersPlus, 13 is the Alpha and Omega, the beginning and the end. Many ancient secret societies and mystery schools understood that the number 13 represented death and rebirth through ascension into eternal life and it represented the secret knowledge of all life including sacred sexuality. It is synchronistic that the 13th card in the Tarot is the Death card and the 13th rune in the Norse alphabet "Eiwaz" is also linked with the balance between light and dark, death and rebirth, the Heavens and the Underworld.

For many of us, sexual traumas taught us early on how to hide and disguise divine power, due to the need to protect or safeguard "that" which has its being in each and every one of us, including men. Men also inherently possess this feminine power (much like estrogen and testosterone existing in both men and women), and are also taught at a young age to mask it underneath false manhood, either through the same offenses or other forms of control. The misconception is that feminine power has to do with being girly, instead of everything to do with the energy of **creativity, vulnerability, empathy,** and **intuition**; more on this later. The most you and all of us were ever really taught and learned about our bodies was to pour it out on our partners in a marriage or relationship (only after we were told to hold on to it and wait for "the one"), have babies with it, and/or suppress it through traumas like those mentioned above. Was there anyone to tell you that there were more powerful things to do with your body other than just intercourse, and other than through it being taken unwillingly? Hell, no! Hence the onset of what is called anxiety and depression for many appear to be the symptoms of something much more *pressing* (literally).

I've allowed the "**all knowing**" to again channel through me in order to communicate this concept with you more deeply. As usual, I can only share this insight with you in the manner in which it is given to and through me from my invisible guides and ancient self.

Downloaded/Uploaded/Intuitively Channeled Message

These particular mental health disorders show up merely to say, "There is misunderstood, and/or misused power hidden away inside of you waiting to be accessed, activated, and integrated. It is beating at the doors within you trying to communicate that it is done with being usurped, sold, or stolen. Journey through the darkness of yourself, the parts you were taught to vilify to reach this power. Travel into the darkness within and *earn* the keys of wisdom about this power, then do the inner work to raise this power up into your higher mind and body. It is trapped and waiting for you to set it free. This is where you gain your mental stability, emotional intelligence, and freedom.

—The All

Chapter 3: Mental Disorders & Suppressed Feminine Power

My experiences with anxiety, depression, and suicidal thoughts showed themselves to be something much more profound than mere diagnoses. So I confidently opted out of seeking clinical opinions. I knew I was being guided to dive deeper into my own mind, body, and emotions to reveal something much more than most traditional approaches would or even could explore. I was determined to uncover the hidden "other" truths about what anxiety, depression, and suicidal thoughts really were, and why they showed up *for me* at all. I was more keen on figuring out what this phenomenon was that affected the mind and body of not just me, but of countless women, men, and children (especially girls) around the world. An anomaly that has been perpetually suppressed throughout the ages of painful experiences and misguided information. In my search, I was led to uncover a one-word truth like an epiphanic revelation, and that word was ***Power!***

Downloaded/Uploaded/Intuitively Channeled Message

To you they said, hide your power deep inside of you, lest you be killed for the crime of being not a witch; but a woman naturally born with spiritual abilities said to be from the devil. Hide your powers deep inside of you, and let no one access it unless he is your husband. If you are beautiful, choose to go against being owned by way of marriage by he who wishes to enslave you, choose to speak up for yourself, and challenge set norms of a woman's role in a man's world, then ye be a witch and killing by way of hanging, and burning be your punishment.

—The All, Feminine Goddess, The Ancient Ones

As I journeyed through the darkness of my own mind and body to uncover why anxiety and depression showed up for me, I realized that not only was I journeying through my inner darkness (shadow-work) to recover and heal fragments of what is known as the inner-child, and ancestral trauma and/or generational curses, but that I was also getting to know a power (a consciousness) that I had not been introduced to before. An energy that although had been hidden and shunned away, was **confident, sure of itself and what it had to offer the world**—an energy that was **magnetic, charming, fiery, sensual, sensitive,** and absolutely **sexy!** The thing is, these aspects were the **exact** opposite of what mental health disorders are described as, right? How could I be addressing the rising up of angst, only to discover that what I thought was anxiety was actually trapped power begging to be **acknowledged, respected**, and **activated**? How could I be addressing the sinking feeling of depression, only to find that I was pressing in (**de =** down, away **/ pressing =** bear down on, lower, hold down) what I was taught to fear? I found myself at a never-before-seen juncture between healing what I thought was *pain* and discovering what was actually power.

I meditated long and diligently on this part of the Activate because I knew I was being guided to exposing these hidden-in-the-dark truths on the link between mental health disorders and suppressed feminine power (a.k.a. divine energy). Let's examine the characteristics of feminine power (i.e., energy) by taking a deep dive into exactly what feminine principles are. We'll also examine what feminine power looks like when stuck, and when divinely activated based on qualities displayed in a person.

Activate

Feminine Principles or Characteristics

- Intuition
- Health
- Heart
- Right side of the brain
- Charm & beauty
- Sensual & sexy
- Empathy
- Birthing
- Creative & artsy
- Vulnerable
- Fiery & passionate

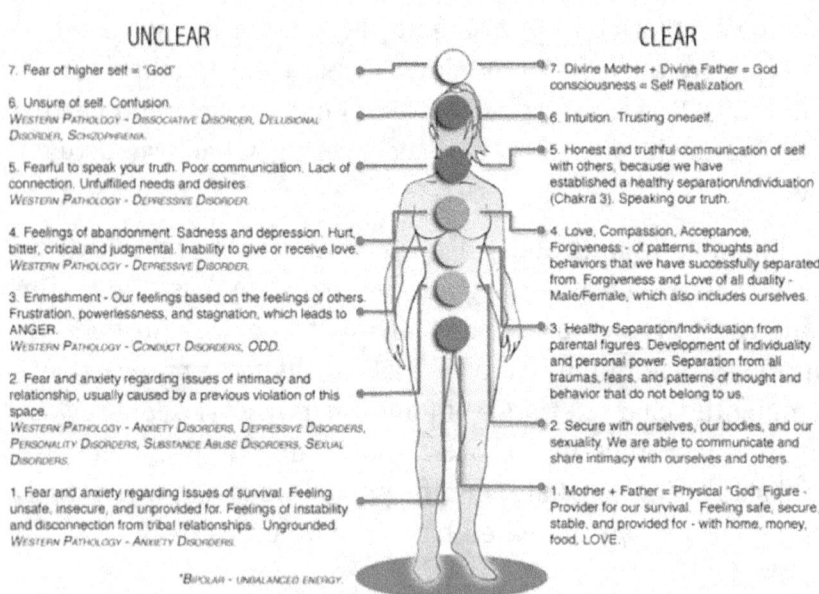

Photo taken from Psychodynamic and Spiritual Awakening Counseling (psychodynamicawakening.com)

I included this photo in **Chapter Two: Mental Disorder and Sexual Trauma**. I'm including it again to drive home why, when, where, and how we began to suppress, hide, and mask feminine energy. Notice the image above as it relates to the red, orange and yellow chakra centers of the body and their descriptions when clear and unclear. When feminine power is stuck, hidden, or misused in the exploitation of sex in these three areas, the person may exhibit the following behaviors:

- Fear, anxiety, depression regarding issues of survival
- Fear regarding issues of intimacy and relationships usually caused by a previous violation of this space (i.e., sexual trauma)
- Feeling unsafe and insecure
- **POWERLESSNESS**

I'm sure by now you know all too well why I bolded "powerlessness"; but just in case you don't let me say it out loud for the people in the back (in the back of your head that is) . . . YES! You are indeed powerless, contrary to the usual "Pollyanna" commentary that you are strong and beautiful. You are powerless not in the notion that you do not have power, but in the sense that you have been taught to give it away—or allow it to be stolen away! Because your power is being given or stolen away as opposed to being fully activated, you experience extreme levels of mental disorders such as anxiety and depression. "**Anxiety and depression for most women is suppressed feminine power that is screaming to be unleashed**" is a mental health philosophy I created and live by to date. When we consider the 16th and 17th century witch hunts (*i.e., crimes against all women and not just the ones doing the low vibrational shit for selfish gains*), we can pretty much draw a straight line from the development of mental and emotional disorders in women from then to the present day. The suppression of feminine power wasn't just an act against wicked witches (*i.e.,*

mentally and emotionally ill women who played around with the power of alchemy to attack others due to their own lowly activated vibrations), but a stint designed to teach all women (and men) who just so happened to be beautiful, had empathic abilities, clairvoyance, and fiery passion about the things she/he cared about, to hide, give away, and sell away their power or face being charged with the crime of being a pseudo witch and sentenced to death in the most excruciating way imaginable.

Now remember as previously mentioned, mental disorders are vastly different from mental illnesses in this particular body of work. Mental disorder (dis-order) suggests that there is hidden power *out of order* and out of its rightful place within you, but mental *illness* displayed through a purposeful attempt to use alchemy (spell work) to harm others, is a sickness within the mind and emotions of the person, who more than likely must be treated with clinical support and doctor-prescribed medications.

Mental disorders, on the other hand, are the symptoms of a lack of power flow from the lower to the higher chakra centers. Why? Because power or what is called "sexual" energy, which in turn is really "feminine characteristics," are not being activated to move/channel to the higher chakra centers. Meaning, the inner mind, heart, voice, and soul are starving because of the energy they are not receiving. Starving the higher self and mind, and only feeding the lower-self results in power held hostage in the lower bodies due to fear of persecution by those with mental illness. Hence, the onset or increase of disorder in the mind and emotions. Disorder simply means, energy that is out of order, **not "in" motion, stuck, hidden, stagnant, suppressed**, and/or **misused** (i.e., sexual exploitation).

According to Blomquist in *Rehabilitating the Witch*,

> Broedel writes that defining witches according to sexualized criteria allowed Sprenger and Kramer

to create a new conceptual field in which . . . sexuality [was] identified with the devil, inverted gender roles and sexual dysfunction with witchcraft, and defective social and political hierarchies with women and women's sins." In his study of the visual representation of witches, Lorenzo Lorenzi links accusations of witchcraft to female sexuality and argues that the women accused of witchcraft were the women who challenged male interests. He writes, "As demi-goddess, mater matuta, artificer, disrupter of the male hierarchy of power, she attracted widespread interest as a woman seeking to assert her feminine being by using all the tools at her disposal, her psychic powers and her charm and beauty, the latter being the vehicle for conveying her sexuality" (Blomquist, 40-41).

In reference to the above quote on witchcraft links to women who challenged male interests and so-called "inverted gender roles," meaning certain women who desired to take on male-driven positions of power and profession, I was yet again given another downloaded, uploaded, and activated channeled message to share with those of you who've decided to pick up this book. I can only give it how it is given to me.

Downloaded/Uploaded/Intuitively Channeled Message

The rise of the feminine does not seek to challenge male interests, it does however dispel ANY toxicity that seeks to poison the minds and hearts of all people; rather those poisons are displayed in males, females, or a cross between the two. In fact, what may have been a challenge of male interests was really the seed of the suppressed feminine beginning to take root, desiring to rise within not just women but in men, as well. However, many of your kind purposely *smite* the seed of the "she" within before it had the chance to activate fully into power. Because of her evolution, she has learned to only choose to be with, live with, love, and align with the new-age men of substance who have done the same inner dark work to also rise, as they are the mirrors of her risen self. She does not seek to challenge those who have decided to fear her to prove she's worthy; she simply begins to mirror and attract those that already know she is. She refuses to debate or argue with anyone about anything that seeks to question her power, because she knows that her truth needs no proof when she is already a walking, talking, living, breathing demonstration of her power. The common misconception is that women who rise in their divine feminine power seek to overthrow men, this could not be FURTHER from the truth if it is TRUE POWER. True power that rises up through the fires of activation despises the idea of trying to overpower. It is instead <u>aroused</u> by unification. True power realizes that both counterparts are needed and wanted. In fact, risen power finds it absolutely sexy when all parts are fully activated. They both know that a bird cannot fly on one wing, meaning taking flight cannot happen without both powers fully *erect*. When someone has taken the journey through the darkness of her own mind and emotions and has risen her fires to be crowned, she is well aware of how serious her purpose is, and respects, honors, and worships those who have traveled down that same path of alchemical activation. They then are once again, fully integrated and activated as infinite parts of the same whole. This is the journey where the previously hunted/haunted unleashes her once suppressed warrior— in the event that she must slay while in the *action* of protecting herself and loved ones from those hunting/haunting to kill, steal, and destroy her again.

—The Ancestors, The All, The Ancient Ones, Divine Feminine, Divine Masculine

Timmesha Burgess

According to Rehabilitating the Witch,

> Witches were women who seduced men and led them down sensual and corrupting paths of sin. Their view of witches was a chilling and intriguing allusion to that of Eve in the Garden of Eden. Like Eve offering an apple to Adam and thereby prompting his sin, the two Dominicans believed that witches were the worldly link that connected the Devil to men. They suggested that the Devil could not operate without "the assistance of some agent" and claimed that he needed these Eves/witches to fulfill his evil tasks. They maintained that witches succeeded in corrupting men because they were "beautiful to look at" and "contaminating to the touch" with voices that "entice passersby and kill them . . . by causing them to forsake God (Blomquist, 37-38)

As I read this chapter of Blomquist's thesis, a light came on not only in my mind, but in my heart and in my womb. Another intuitive channeled message raised up inside of me with deep revelation that follows.

> **Downloaded/Uploaded/Intuitively Channeled Message**
>
> It was the woman (who just so happened to be esthetically beautiful) that questioned religious doctrine, traditions, beliefs, practices, and questioned so-called leaders about their leadership. Her boldness threatened their plans for domination and power. It was the empathic woman who shed light on the lies, deceit, and the evil schemes that their husbands, friends, and families couldn't see, but that her dreams, visions, and intuition could. It was the woman that warned and consulted with her husband about the hidden agendas he couldn't see. She was a threat to the God that "they created" and wanted everyone to believe in. Therefore, she was a threat to their plan of controlling the minds and hearts of all people. She, her beauty and her spiritual gifts had to be stopped, by forcing her into submission with fear, and with the projection of witch onto her identity forever and ever...by any means necessary!"
>
> **—The Ancestors, The All**

In my research, there were numerous accounts that pointed to some men who were married or otherwise involved romantically who were publicly caught with another, or committing what the church would call "adultery." In chapter one, I mentioned how when a woman or girl was raped and became pregnant, that the assailant would blame her for getting pregnant and of witchcraft. When in fact, her pregnancy was the proof that would render him the culprit instead. Therefore, the blame had to be that she was a witch that caused him to force his way not only onto but INTO her.

As it relates to beauty, sensuality, sexuality, and allegations of her that caused men to forsake God, one could ascertain that the criminal acts against women were purely forged from a desire for power and control of more than just women, but of an ever present source of God known as the **feminine principle**. Feminine principles of God or *Goddess* embody the characteristics of **attraction, sensuality, sexuality, inner and outer beauty, intuitive gifts, empathic abilities,** and **clairvoyance**. Therefore, if and when a woman (or man) embodies these qualities, she/he is actually displaying the qualities of God *herself.* Popular religious doctrine teaches that God has only ever been Father God or God the Father; therefore, when the feminine God qualities showed themselves present in the actions of both women and men (outside of the norm for indoctrinated teachings), it /she/her is said to be of the devil, and of witchcraft instead of something much more omnipresent.

For example, I am a dreamer—I don't mean dreamer in the sense that I simply dream of one day doing something and going somewhere, but literal during sleep prophetic dreams pertaining to my life and existence at large. Meaning when I sleep I travel to alternate realms of consciousness, subconsciousness, and unconsciousness, and I receive numerous visions from places I've never visited and people I've never met, well at least not in this lifetime. Now my mother happens to be a POWERFUL dream interpreter, who should actually be called dream decoder because she possesses the gift of interpreting dreams like the character in the Bible named David. We've often conversed jokingly saying, "***Hey, do you know if we lived back in the day that we'd be accused of being witches and killed?***" While we can joke about that now, the seriousness of this is that it is absolutely true! Considering the amount of women and girls who embody these spiritual gifts naturally helps to shed light on the number of them that suppress them due to fear, even today! Can you imagine having dreams and visions, and having no one around that can help you understand them? Can you imagine being a person that can interpret and decode spiritual insight but having to stay quiet

Activate

due to fear for your life? Hence the onset and the rise of what we call anxiety and depression.

Do you possess a natural gift that you were born with such as intuitive insight or clairvoyance? Do you have dreams when you sleep at night and visions during the day that you can't explain to anyone around you? If so, jot down what you think they are trying to tell you on the page below. Refer back to this page whenever you feel the rise of anxiety, depression, or suicidal thoughts rise within you. It will help guide you towards the work you must do to set yourself free.

_____

_____

_____

_____

_____

_____

_____

_____

_____

_____

_____

_____

_____

_____

When I read this passage from Blomquist: "They maintained that witches succeeded in corrupting men because they were 'beautiful to look at' and 'contaminating to the touch' with voices that 'entice passersby and kill them,'" I laughed hysterically! Why? Because what came to me was such a revelation on the premise that ignorance produces fear, fear produces hate, and hate produces discrimination. Mama Goddess (aka, Divine Feminine) wants me to write exactly as she gives it, so I can only write what comes to me in the exact form she asks me to write it.

Downloaded/Uploaded/Intuitively Channeled Message

You have created in them a spirit of fear ... not of you, but fear of themselves! You have taught her to seek to be overly humble, not to smile too much or be too sensational, for she'd be a witch and killed. You taught her to vilify her ancient wisdom and intelligence by telling her that she gained it from evil sources. You have taught her to hide and mask her beauty because of your inability to maintain control of your own lower nature; so you blame her. You convinced her that her inner intuition and outer beauty were sins rather than her gifts to create more wellbeing. This has taught her to not only hate herself, but to also despise, hate, and "hate on" any others who display any such beauty. You blame her for your shortcomings, for your lack of self-control, and for your lack in being able to raise your own phallus energy without needing help from her to do so. It is you who lacks the mental and emotional intelligence to raise your energy from your lower bodies into your higher minds. You have projected your own mental illness onto her, and she accepted this because she thought it was your love for her. She now knows what to do to regain her crown and reoccupy her throne. NO ONE and NO THING will hinder her again, lest she hinders herself. Her hindrance will not be because of you ... not anymore; but of her own delay in gaining and refining her mental health, and reorganizing the disorder of

> ancient, disseminated information hidden in the darkness of her own mind and body. Amen and AWOMEN.
>
> ## — Divine Feminine, Mama Goddess, The Ancient Ones, The All, The Ancestors

> ***SIDE BAR:*** *At the very moment I was writing the previous channeled message, I paused to say "Damn, talk yo shit through me, Mama Feminine God, TALK YO SHIT TO THEM THEN!" Because even as I write every word of this book, I too am being schooled and further activated.*

Truth Moment: When I would receive visions or huge revelations, I would quickly write them down in my dream or **"things I want to remember"** journal. I was in the process of searching for something in particular for the next chapter of this manual in my journal, but my eyes caught a revelation I wrote down in June 2020. I'm including this because it's important to share with you what it looked like for me when I gathered the breadcrumbs that led the way to when, where, why, and how I began to hide, disguise, and suppress my feminine principles day to day. So much so, that it negatively affected how I romantically interacted with men. I hid what I thought was too much or somehow too attractive. In my journal I wrote the following:

Dancing Meditation/Strawberry full moon

I am remembering a time when I was dating a guy named (undisclosed for legal reasons). His mental health (***really should've said illness***) *I allowed to affect my mental health. I am remembering how angry he would be when I smiled at people. I smiled at everyone . . . including guys, kids, animals. He used to raise his voice at me in private, but would be extremely loving in public around his peers. So I stopped smiling at men because of what I allowed from him. Today I set myself free from that emotional and mental memory and energy tether. I release that from being buried . . . and I choose to open myself back up to smiling at men again.*

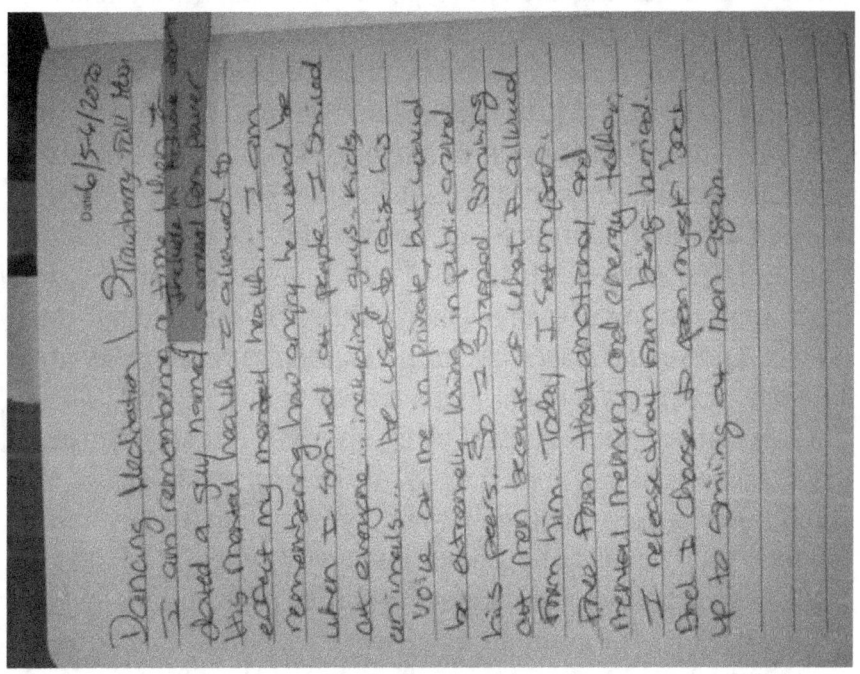

Photo taken from inside one of my dream & vision journals.

This dating experience among many others taught me to hold my head down most of the time, and avoid eye contact with others. It taught me to shrink and to be submissive not to the man but to abusive misuse of power. This negatively affected my ability to enjoy romantic relationships or even allow myself to enter them without fear that I would do something to offend him.

Now let's not be naive or dismissive of the fact that there were those that purposely chose and still choose to harm others by forcing their power or attempting to take others powers through malicious attacks and sorcery. Yes, people can and will do really fucked-up things to one another when mental and emotional health is lacking. Because as I mentioned before, there were and still are a number of women and men that instead of accessing their God powers to end wars choose to wield their powers to begin them (I did mention spell work in chapter one). The use of alchemy to harm others was very real then as it is today, just take a look around at the past few centuries to this present day! The mistake that the majority of humans made was propagating the belief that anyone who was tapped into their feminine God power were all evil and nothing more. THIS WAS A HUGE MISTAKE, and has been the sole detriment to the fall of man *over* and *over* and *over* again. Man (**Man: A perpetual masculine term designed to envelope all of the human race**) didn't just *fall* once according to biblical interpretations thousands of years ago. NO! But still continues to fall every single day due to purposeful subjugation that repudiates a part of the human psyche and of the human experience, from that of the feminine principle of God, aka, the suppression of **feminine power**. Before attacks among people, countries, or nations could ever exist, a war first had to begin *within* the human mind and body, because the ultimate divide of one's own self-perception breeds chaos.

Ever wonder why when taught to pray, we were told to end with Amen? Well I did! As I began my journey through the darkness (hidden/shadow) parts of my own mind and emotions to uncover why anxiety and depression showed up so strongly for me, I questioned ABSOLUTELY EVERYTHING about what I had been taught, and more so, what I had not been taught. I thought about how disrespectful and heartbreaking it is to all that is feminine to forge such a divide between the masculine and feminine and only honor and recognize the masculine. My question then became, "Why shouldn't I say both Amen and Awomen? Because I know that this earth and everything in it is built on the **natural law** of duality, i.e., the sun and moon, yin and yang, day and night/shadow, Father God, but where is Mama God? Where has the feminine principle been hiding, or better yet, where has she been hidden? I'll tell you where . . . IN THE DARK. She's been hidden in the deepest, darkest parts of our minds and our bodies for so long, that she now shows up in us as what we call **anxiety** and **depression**. When I ponder this idea of a longstanding masculine figure but the removal of the feminine figure, I can as an empath sense the heartbreak of every mother who's birthed children on this planet. Why? Because I've imagined carrying, nurturing, feeding, growing, and caring for an entire human in my body—giving birth to him or her, and them never even knowing I existed. Not because I wasn't there or didn't love them well, but because I was locked away in the deepest of darks and was never even mentioned to him/her AT ALL!

I remember sharing this concept once with a young woman who was the mother of a seven-year-old boy. In our first in-depth conversation, she went on and on about how Father God this and her Father God that, so much so that I was activated to respond in a way neither one of us expected. I said to her, "*You're a mother right . . . can you imagine having done all you've done to care for and birth your son and him never even knowing you exist? Can you imagine his father getting all the honor and not you? I wonder why we allow this in our spiritual beliefs? Why have we been taught to acknowledge a Father God, but never a Mother God?*" She looked down with a confused, sad, yet perplexed look on her face—and it was at that very moment she realized that she too had been removed from "her" story (history). As you read that yourself, can you feel a deep sense of sadness? Can you feel the voice of some unknown, echoed cry for help from within? If so, then this is your proof as to why anxiety, depression, and suicidal thoughts have shown up for you. Disorder in your mind and body is your proof of the hidden and dismissed feminine within us all, beckoning us to honor her existence and formidable power.

I mean, we have accepted the feminine in aspects of birthing as the female who brings forth life from the spirit world into the physical world through her body, we've accepted calling our planet "mama" Earth as she also births and brings forth life when we plant seeds into her fertile soil, when the skies pour out rain to water the crops and produce food to nourish our families, plants, and animals we pray and ask "mother" nature to take its course right? So, when and why have we decided to negate, ignore, vilify, hide in the shadows, and make demonic "Mama" as it relates to God? How is it that God without the feminine gave birth to "the all" alone? Because this realm of existence on planet earth is built on the natural law of duality . . . wouldn't this suggest that there must be a Mother God? An equal and as power counterpart that helped to birth forth creation?

Speaking of creation, doesn't the act of creation, i.e., creativity itself, have to do with the feminine principle, with creativity being one of the primary characteristics of femininity and feminine power? One would begin to deeply feel the wicked schemes behind the suppression of the feminine and why now more than ever, people are waking up to the truth, to the truth of not only what has been done to enslave minds, but enslave individual power, and enslave the feminine energy in the darkness. When we think about the negative impacts on women throughout time, it is clear that women's and girls' sexual abuse, economic impacts, workforce biases, unequal pay, so on and so forth— has much less to do with just women and more so to do with the continuous attacks on the existence of the feminine presence.

Mental health disorders didn't just arise from day-to-day experiences such as relationships that end, job losses, or losing a loved one, but established its roots at the precipice of the suffrage of not just women, but of the feminine essence of God or Goddess itself. Think about it . . . No, **FEEL** into this wisdom right now as you read this! If you come from a family or culture whose beliefs are rooted in church doctrine, the traditional concept of God has always been taught as masculine father God, male Jesus the savior, and a male Holy Spirit. With the generational teachings of religiosity, and even in most adopted forms of language, the use of masculine terms such as *he*, *him*, and *you guys* further solidify the oppression of any and all references that are even remotely feminine in nature. Thus perpetuating generational cycles on a species of women, females, and feminine energy (also existing in men) who see no reflection of themselves or their power anywhere—not even in God. Well DAMN! The question for me then became, "**How can I possibly know myself when I can't even see myself in the one that 'supposedly' loves, guides, and created me?**"

When I meditated on exactly what the term "mental disorder" meant and how this correlates with the dismissal, suppression, or removal of the feminine essence of God (Divine Feminine), I was channeled yet another message from ancestors, light and dark angels, and spirit/invisible guides. As always I can only share this in the way they gave it to me.

Downloaded/Uploaded/Intuitively Channeled Message

What you call a mental disorder is really a disorder of disseminated information in your mind and body. Your ancient wisdom and intelligence is out of order, out of its RIGHTFUL place within your psyche and body. Disorder means the state of confusion or to make chaos the systematic functioning of something. That "something" is who and what you really are, and the power you truly possess to heal yourself and others. Your mind is only in disorder because instead of your power being in its **rightful place**, it is hidden, tucked and pushed away into the darkest parts of your psyche. To regain order, mental order (i.e., mental health), you must reawaken the knowledge locked away within you, and put it back in its rightful place. Disorder persists because you continue to mask the shadow part of your consciousness that gives birth—the feminine. This causes a divide in you rather than integration of all the infinite parts of you. You have been torn into two—one half has been hidden away in the dark. This hidden half of you is banging at the doors within, in hopes that it again will be recognized, seen, loved, respected, protected, and rescued by you and you alone. When she is risen, as you have risen "he," an integral love story begins again. A sexy dance between the masculine and the feminine.

—The All, The Ancients Ones

> ***SIDE BAR:*** *In this next portion I was guided to remove all of my clothes and spread my legs for better channeling of the messages that follow in this chapter. Why? Because the ancient wisdom awakening within me needed my body to be clear of anything that could hinder the free flow of communication through and around me. I allowed myself to feel aroused from the information that made its way through and out of me. Had I not been aroused, I would not have been able to share this ancient insight with you. You will know why arousal was absolutely imperative for this part after reading below.*

I again must speak from the higher and lower sources that communicate through me to you (and to me as well). While I was in meditation, I had yet another vision of the inside of my body. As I was being taken down into my lower, dark/shadow self, goddess **Qetesh**, *nature goddess of sacred ecstasy and sexual pleasure,* began teaching me. I must speak it exactly the way in which it was said to me, so here goes; the consciousness of Goddess Katesh channels through me says:

Downloaded/Uploaded/Intuitively Channeled Message

Sensual and sexual energy is planted in the root chakra like a seed that is supposed to grow and rise. So many of you have not been properly taught how to nourish this inner-seed power for growth.

Many of you have stunted your energy seed in your root by continuously pouring it out in unfulfilling relationships, or it's being stolen, bought or sold through sexual exploitation. The work for what you call "sensual" and "sexual" energy is to water and nourish it, so that it can grow to rise into all other parts of your body and mind. You only call it sexual because that's the only place you have stored and activated this energy until this point. You have refused to grow it from there. You are not only aroused to then get rid of your arousal, you are to honor the energy that shows up in the emotion of arousing, and grow it upward. You cannot be completely removed from the root's dark, because it is your soil, to try to negate your dark root is **futile**. Grow power through the dark soil of your root, through your body, up and out of your crown chakra . . . like a tree. This is the idea of raising energy up from the lower to the higher, from dark to light for integration. Forever and always being rooted in the dark wombs root soil—like a tree on your earth, then growing out and bursting through the crown. It is being crowned up there, YOU ARE BEING CROWNED when you raise the energy up to the head/mind/crown chakra. The body is the throne and the head is the crown. When your sensual and sexual energy rises from the lower to the higher, it reaches the crown thus gaining its crown. Grow your sensual and sexual energy like a tree through your body, up and out of your crown. That is the work in which to gain your mental and emotional health, intelligence, and stability. This is how you sit boldly on your throne—the throne of you, with your crown, and in your own power... knowing what you are here to do as ruler and leader of yourself.

— Goddess Qetesh, The Divine, The Dark, The Light, The All

In the midst of focusing on growing my energy from seed into a full tree to be crowned (as revealed in the channeled message), I was again shown an image in my mind's eye. The following picture is a drawing that my higher self showed to me while I was focusing on raising my seed power into my mind and body.

The image I saw in my mind's eye reflects that once your seed-power is watered to grow, your power will begin to produce fruit. Fruit that you get to enjoy yourself and share with those around you. How do you water your seed-power for growth?

1. Inner dark work that addresses what lives beneath the trauma. This may be done with someone you ABSOLUTELY TRUST, who has also traveled the dark journey and knows the ropes (sort of speak) over a long-period of time. This work is a lifetime process of continuous evolution.
2. Specific inner healing methods such as but not limited to ancient yoga poses, detoxing, fasting, crystal applications, and sound therapy that targets the lower-base chakras to dissolve blocked energy. This work is done like the building blocks of foundation, from the base working your way up as described from root chakra, raising the energy from the root to the crown.
3. Feeding the mind and body new philosophies that will begin to re-activate the powers of the lower chakras, to fully rise up again to the crown chakra to be crowned.
4. Number four is an activated, download/upload message. As usual, I can only offer it as it is activated within me through my spiritual guides; so here goes.

Downloaded/Uploaded/Channeled Message in response to #4

There is a misconception about the activation of the suppressed seed-power, i.e., Goddess and Divine Feminine energy. It isn't this pretty image of rainbows, sunshine, butterflies, and frolicking about in fields of flowers. It is not merely the wearing of shiny jewelry, dancing about, and putting on pretty clothes. It is not the display of what "looks like" feminine energy, Quite the contrary! Rather, it is the "BEing" of it.

If there is anyone that teaches false ideas on how to become more or tap into Goddess/Feminine Energy, or become more attractive by playing, dancing, wearing

this, doing that, those are your false prophets. How? Because true power knows that there must be the inner *undoing* before there can be an outer doing. Those who have truly taken this journey to activate their suppressed feminine power know that there must be a journey into the underworld, into the dark, because that is where Goddess dwells. To activate her is actually not a walk in the park, nor is it fun, and nor is it for the faint of heart—it is a journey down into the rabbit hole.

You cannot get to the concept of play, dance, moving your hips, and wearing displays of tingling jewelry until you first journey through the dark. Your beauty on the surface will be inevitable if you do the inner dark work of raising your suppressed power up for activation; the outer will shift NO MATTER WHAT, and it will have less to do with what you wear. The Goddess, and divine femininity, cannot be worn like yet another mask or costume. You will know the dark Goddess is activated in someone when they enter a room based on the energy they carry from within.

Anyone who attempts to guide you on tapping into your divine, suppressed feminine energy or Goddess by telling you to

> simply play, dance, and frolic around disgraces her and disrespects the profundity of what it, this, she truly is. This confusion has been to the detriment of those of you on this journey of uncovering what mental disorders truly are for you. You find yourselves wearing yet another mask of falsehood, Pollyanna, rainbows and butterflies; therefore, inner mental and emotional suffering continues because there is still no true activation of your suppressed power.
>
> When you take the journey through the inner tumultuous dark to access, activate, and unleash her, ONLY THEN will you dance, play, frolic, and place outward crowns upon your head, around your wrists, ankles, and necks. Why?
>
> 1. Because your outward crowns will symbolize your inner work to raise your energy up into your crown chakra.
> 2. Your jewelry will symbolize adornment of your internal alchemy of turning led to gold.
> 3. And your dance will be the celebration that you survived the darkness to unleash, to activate, and to rise. Your dancing and frolicking will be symbolic of your victory. Your decision to always dance will be for celebratory reasons that no one will know but you—but you will know that you have taken and risen through the dark journey within to earn your stripes as the beautiful warrior.
>
> ## —The Divine Feminine

Disorder comes when the seed has been stolen through sexual trauma, bought through forced sexual relationships, or improperly activated through exploited sexual acts. When the power seed is able to fully grow, it can produce infinitely more fruit for the well-being of all involved. However, when the seed is stolen or sold, mental disorder continues because of the lack of nourishment and growth into higher levels. Thus no production of fruit (*i.e., health, love, empathy, mental and emotional health, creativity, intuition, nation building*) ensues, imbalance incurs, and disorder within the mind and body continues. In the event your seed is taken over and over again through sexual abuse, or through your own purposeful misuse via exploitation or purely sexual attachments, the true power remains trapped and inactivated. It remains trapped where the trauma takes place—in the root—the opening to your womb and power, thus showing up as anxiety and depression. Your **power seed** is not properly nourished by your work in raising it into your higher mind and chakras; it remains stunted underneath the surface, trapped where the exploitation takes place (the entry to the vagina and womb)—forever showing up as disorder in the body and mind.

Allow my sketch in the following section to act as a lens into your own inner body, showing you where your feminine power lay trapped, hidden, misused, and/or abused.

Timmesha Burgess

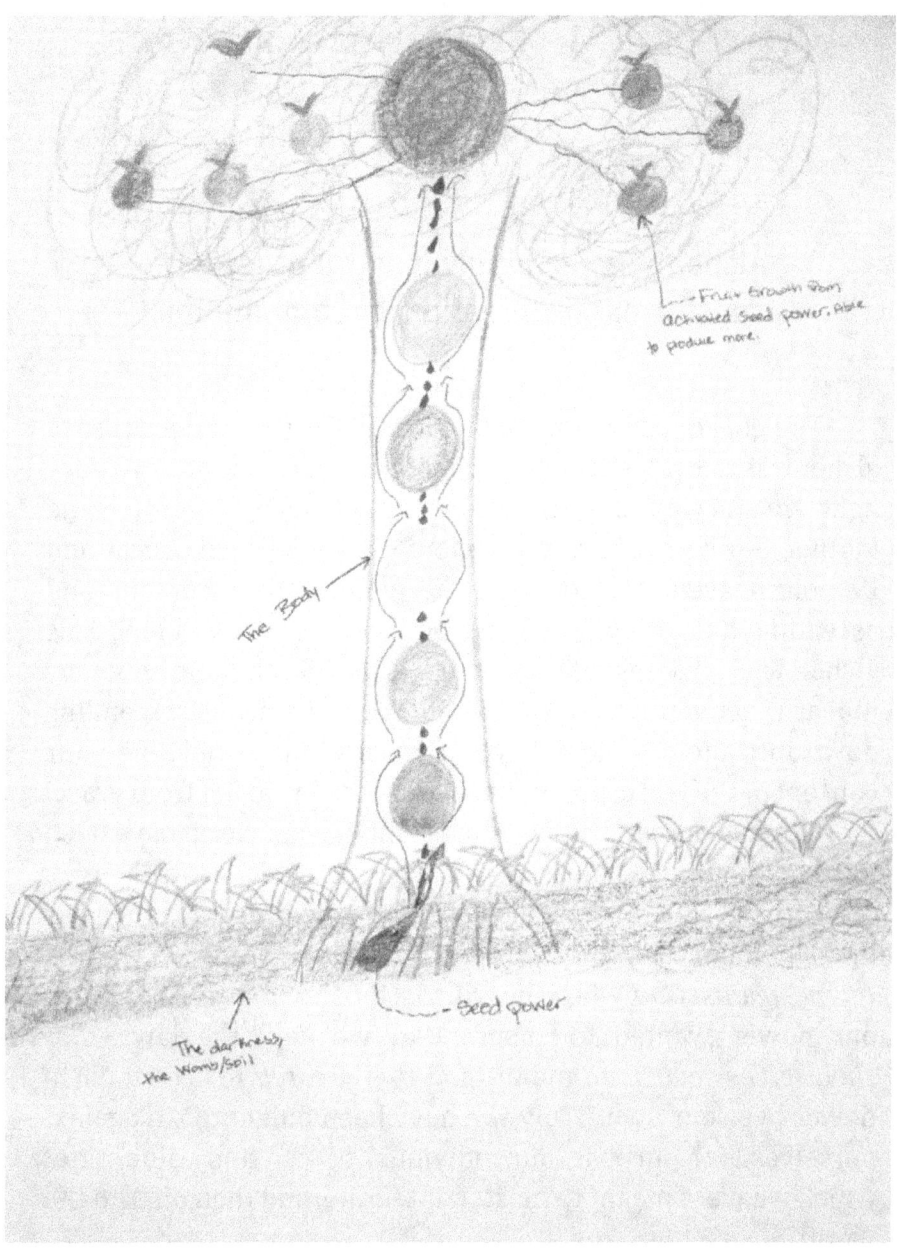

Vision sketch of suppressed seed power risen, activated, unleashed by Timmésha Burgess.

CHAPTER 4: MENTAL DISORDERS & THE ALCHEMICAL PROCESS

Alchemy; a seemingly magical process of transformation, creation, or combination.

The goal of activating mental health through the process of alchemy is to bridge together or integrate your darkness to your light, yin and yang, sun and moon, day and night, father God and Mother Goddess, above and below, God and Devil, Angel and Demon, heaven and hell. It is the process of descending and ascending like an infinite dance between heaven and hell. This alchemical process allows you to efficiently and divinely unleash, activate, and operate your superpower. Descending down into the darkness of you requires you to redefine your concept of the word sin; because to sin means to fall from grace; therefore, to descend equals sin, meaning what we all have been taught about the meaning of sin, in and of itself is a transgression against us all. This **play on words** has taught us that sinning means to *do wrong*, *break laws*, to *misbehave*, and *offend against God*, when the truth is, those who sought to usurp our power wanted to ensure that we kept the laws *they themselves developed* and the god *they created,* to keep them in power over our own. Truly, we have been taught to sin against ourselves, our purpose, our individual power, and value, all of which we were meant to master, integrate, and then offer to the world.

I discovered that what I thought was pain was really the symptoms of something much more *powerful* wanting to be fully activated and set free. This idea of freeing and activating this power, however, could not happen without the wisdom, application, and surrender to the process of inner alchemy. I like to look at the journey through the darkness of mental health as a three-part alchemical journey. A journey through alchemical phases in which I call **Twilight**, **Dusk**, and **Dawn**, which I'll talk more in-depth about later. These phases are the points of inner cosmic *initiation* in which you journey down into the great darkness (i.e., your inner hell or underworld) to gather your hidden treasures, forge a relationship with your inner demons, then rise back up again fully activated in your power. But this time having integrated both your dark and light, angels and demons, God and Devil, heaven and hell, and your masculine and feminine selves, through the process of *alchemical-activation* from within.

So what exactly is this idea of alchemy? Well according to Jungian theory:

- Alchemy is a personal journey of transformation and an instinctive impulse for growth.
- People with an inflexible mind and a consciousness that focuses merely on objectives, material things, and the observable will have a limited life.
- To favor a broader and higher consciousness like Isaac Newton's, we must develop, according to Jung, the following four alchemical elements: Fire (feeling, choleric), Water (thinking, phlegmatic), Air (intuition, sanguine), and Earth (melancholic, sensation).
- Also, psychology and alchemy arise from many of your unresolved psychic elements. You must delve deep into that alchemical darkness where your shadows meet in order to bring them back to light. Every transformation requires effort, open-mindedness, and creativity.

> "There are two kinds of alchemy. One strives to get to know the cosmos as a whole and recreate it. It's the precursor of modern natural science. The other alchemy focuses on the possibility of a transformation that will lead you to be your true self" (Carl Jung, *Psychology and Alchemy*).

To drive home the mission of this book for those of you on this journey of uncovering exactly what anxiety, depression, and suicidal thoughts are for you and why they showed up at all, let's just focus on the latter part of Jungian theory on alchemy relating to "**transformation that will lead to your true self.**" In later chapters, we will touch on the importance of some very *basic* elements of the cosmos and your particular journey through the darkness of you—basically a simplified version of the cosmos and you. Because if we were to dive *completely* into the cosmos relative to this body of work, this book would be the length of an encyclopedia... doubled.

> "For the alchemist the one primarily in need of redemption is not man, but the deity who is lost and sleeping in matter. Only as a secondary consideration does he hope that some benefit may accrue to himself from the transformed substance as the panacea, the medicina catholica, just as it may to the imperfect bodies, the base or "sick" metals, etc. His attention is not directed to his own salvation through God's grace, but to the liberation of God from the darkness of matter." — Carl Jung

The liberation of God from the darkness of matter; how thrilling! As I consider Jung's quote above, I'm being prompted to dig deeper into the history of the **Black Madonna**. Why? Because I had a dream one night that I was at an event, in a ball room filled with people from all over the world—mainly people of Moroccan and Ethiopian bloodlines. In this dream, there was a cake so tall it nearly touched the ceiling, and all the people kept calling the cake, **The Black Madonna**. As I write this portion of **Activate**, I'm being prompted to dig into the concept of the Black Madonna and how it compares to this journey through alchemical activation to liberate God from the darkness of matter for mental health.

According to a piece in Thehistoryofyesterday.com,

> Some scholars, like Stephen Benko, believe that the Black Madonna is an echo of these old religions. The Feminine symbol, and all it represents, was relegated underground. No room whatsoever was left for it on the surface. But it never lost its pulse and it kept sending ripples from the depths . . . There is an overlap in the Christian split between Good and Evil, Man and Woman, Light and Dark. Just like the feminine principles of intuition, subjectivity, and feeling have been labeled as devilish and trickster-like, so have darker colors been associated with the Devil. But this was not always the case. The old religions, just like they recognized the balance between Masculine and Feminine, also recognized the equality between darkness and light. The color black was not seen as evil. It was associated with the night and its proximity to the Divine and the Unconscious. Most of all, however, it was associated with the earth and fertility. The blacker the earth, the more fertile it is. Black was equal to life-giving all-encompassing power. Centuries before chromatics scientists found that

we perceive as black objects that absorb all colors, the ancients already sensed that everything is contained in it ("The Mystery of the Black Madonna").

As I studied the above information and other sources of research, I found my suspicions to be correct relating to not just the color of her skin, but the position of her power. As mentioned above, *the blacker the earth, the more fertile the ground.* Can you recall my mention of the seven stages of seed growth (or how to raise hell) previously? What I innerstand about the concept of the Black Madonna far exceeds even what we consider culture, race or ethnicity to be; instead, her image fortifies the source of darkness in and of itself—or what I like to call, "**the dark side of the sun.**" It has less to do with her skin color and more to do with the essence and the formidable misunderstood power of "the Dark." The question that everyone must ask themselves now is as follows:

- **Do we want to just liberate her "from" the darkness or do we want to *also* liberate darkness itself?**

I say, the time is now to do both! To liberate her from the darkness means to bring her forth from the shadows in which she's been hidden and crown her publicly— and we must also liberate, uphold, honor, and come into oneness with the darkness that she naturally is within us all. Why? Because the darkness in and of itself, is also its own *kind of light.*

Considering Jung's theory on psychology and alchemy and comparing this with the idea of "the fall of man" I previously mentioned in chapter three. A message was again intuitively downloaded, uploaded, and activated through me to share with you relating to the process of alchemy (*dark to light, led to gold, pain to power, disorder to order*). As usual, I must offer it to you exactly how it was given to me, so here goes...

> ### Downloaded/Uploaded/ Intuitively Channeled Message
>
> *The fall*, in and of itself, is synonymous with the descent down from heaven onto the earth realm. This fall down to earth is synonymous with the descent down into the divine darkness of your own earthly mind and body... into your hell/underworld. In this place you will find what was masked and hidden from you. In there, you will find the root of you embedded in the dark womb of the divine dark mother. This you is only dark because that is where you hid a part of yourself... in the dark. Remember the previous image of the tree with its roots planted in the dark ground, but its branches expanding high into the sunlight; it is proof that **like a tree you cannot avoid being rooted in darkness**. You continue to fall into the darkness of who you are for two reasons: **1.** to raise up the powers hidden there, and **2.** to bridge together both your dark and light. You have failed to activate full integration of both your dark and light bodies, because you refuse to honor your dark shadow self, that which is forever rooted in the womb of your hidden dark mother. You fear the dark because of the Devil and demons that live there, when in fact, the Devil and demons are YOU awaiting activation. It is time you learn the truth about darkness contrary to the fears indoctrinated into you about it. You fear the dark because in your existence you were taught that black is bad... from black cats to nighttime, blackmail to black magic. Let us say that even black is as pure as light; however, you have learned to shun it by those who sought to usurp your knowledge of yourself. The term black magic is a play on words, it is not black magic that harms. "DO NOT DISRESPECT THE BLACK DARK BY DEMONIZING ITS NAME"—it is instead "SHIT" MAGIC. Meaning, those with mental illness that choose to harm others with the power of alchemy, purposely waddle in shit to start shit! Let this forever and always be your new definition. You refuse to honor what the darkness offers that assist you with your ascension, so you

> try to avoid going there to your inner dark hell. There is no heaven without first ascending from hell. Your heaven right here on earth. All your life you have been taught to avoid hell (i.e., the darkness and the underworld); however, this is exactly where your journey to activating your full power must take place, and you wonder why your mind and emotions are out of order. There will be no initiation or rise into your higher mind and life's purpose without doing so. Journey into your underworld, and realign with what is there. This is your resurrection, this is how you reorder, recover, and redeem all that is you. This is your redemption.
>
> **— The All**

In the midst of receiving and unlocking this intuitively channeled message, I was shown a vision in my mind's eye, one that I attempted to sketch in the following drawing. A vision that would literally scare the hell (***pun* intended**) out of most people who are not yet on this journey of activation. For the person who has not been called to take this journey, the following image may appear graphic. But not for you, not for the *you* that this is meant for. If it is meant for you, the image will speak to every part of you and the you that is ready to be fully activated through the power of alchemy (i.e., pain to power, lead to gold). You are ready for these beautiful hidden truths into symbolism, visions, and epiphanies that are designed to shatter every false concept that has kept you trapped, and hidden away in the dark.

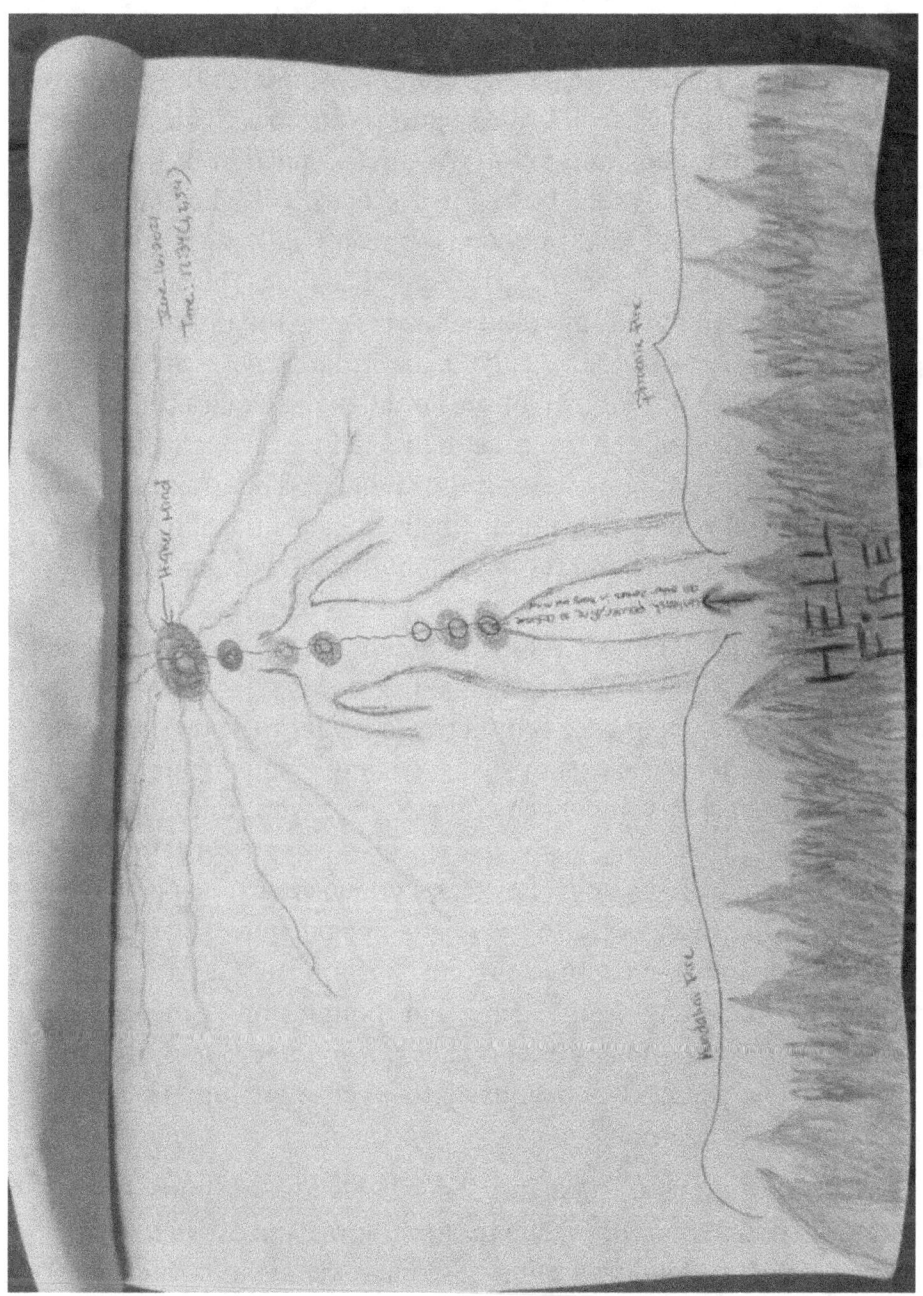

Visual sketch by Timmésha Burgess, representing the descent (fall of man) down into the underworld (i.e., inner darkness, inner hell of the mind and body).

Activate

The wording included in my sketch from left to right reads **Kundalini Fire, Hell Fire, Phoenix Fire**. You'll notice the opening between the legs reads, "**Unleash power/fire to activate all other centers in the body and mind.**" At the top portion of the body where the head would be reads the words "**Higher Mind.**" It shows the crown chakra center (purple) fully activated and extending out for creation, birthing, and healing. This image that was shown to me in my mind's eye reflects the descent down into the underworld (i.e., *fall of man into darkness, inner hell*), to unleash the fire for activation. For all of the chakra centers to be fully activated, the fire must be raised up through the body and out of the crown (inner mind) heaven. The fires have the power to consume and refine. This is the alchemical process as it relates to gaining and refining mental and emotional health—it is the descent or fall down into hell, gaining the keys to unlocking your power, rising or ascending back up into your heaven to be crowned (crown chakra), and to sit on your throne (your body) having been fully activated. Does this story of going to the underworld, gaining keys, and rising again sound familiar? Perhaps the allegorical story we were told about the character Jesus from Western Scriptures rings a bell. However, disorder and illness develops (as I've previously explained in earlier chapters) in those who have not taken or *avoid* taking the inner journey through the darkness to fully activate their chakra bodies with this fire that bubbles underneath the surface. This fire exists as the *primal ingredient* for activation, not to be misused and abused to overpower others or for diabolical schemes.

Unfortunately, this fire has been used, abused, and mistreated for centuries due to the suppression of the feminine principles. The maltreatment of women throughout the ages is merely a reflection of the dismissal of the feminine principle of God/Goddess itself. Anxiety and depression are the symptoms of the continuous attempt to remove the divine dark mother that wishes to be birthed within every human being on this planet. Instead of her having her full birth or rising within our minds and bodies, we are taught to push her back in (*i.e., depress defined as: inhibit, restrict, cut, cheapen, put down, keep down, all which equal depression*), thus inhibiting or should I say ... delaying her rise in power. Promising to never speak to her, hear her, or see her. This was the derivative of "***See No Evil, Hear No Evil, Speak No Evil.***" The human world was taught that the divine goddess hidden in the dark was evil; therefore, do not speak to her, see her, or hear her. These were the early methods that began to split all of humankind away from that which is the source of their power. Imagine, you are pregnant, and the moment it is time for you to give birth, you instead attempt to push the child deeper into your belly—OUCH! However, this is what many are doing every day. By continuing to *depress* that which is meant to be birthed and risen, the suffering of mental, emotional, and physical disorder continues.

According to Wikipedia, Kundalini is defined as the following,

In Hinduism, Kundalini is a form of divine feminine energy believed to be located at the base of the spine, in the muladhara. It is an important concept in Śhaiva Tantra, where it is believed to be a force or power associated with the divine feminine or the formless aspect of the Goddess ... Kundalini is described as a sleeping, dormant potential force in the human organism.

Activate

> ***SIDE BAR:*** *Before continuing into this chapter, I took a quick break. While resting my mind and fingers, I sat on my porch to listen to a YouTube channel I often frequent for motivation. The video is titled* **4 Days of Darkness***. At about 8mins in, the reader Paul Butler, aka Paul White Gold Eagle, channels this message;* **"I am the sacred fire that activates and transforms every cell, every atom, every strand of the DNA."** *It is divine alignment that at this very moment you who are reading this book ... at this very point ... are already fully unleashing your suppressed power, phoenix fire, feminine God, and you are doing the work to raise her back in her rightful position of power. Thus re-ordering, regaining, and refining your mental and emotional health and your life!*

Downloaded/Uploaded/ Intuitively Channeled Message

It was human ego that separated the dark from light, yin from yang, God from Devil, and demon from angel. God never wanted to be separated from Goddess nor separated from devil, it was mental illness that spread like toxicity and poison throughout the minds and hearts of people who created such an illusion, thus causing mental disorder in the masses who were at the mercy of those trusted to lead them. Your fear of Demon is your fear of God in and of itself, and your fear of the darkness is your perpetuated fear of the womb that births you. They taught you to fear the darkness (i.e., the underworld) because they knew it would cause a split in you. Splitting your dark from your light; thus, causing inner chaos and disorder within your mind which you call mental disorder. This was their Trojan horse to get in. To get into your minds and bodies.

—The All

If you are experiencing the onset or increase of mental disorders such as anxiety, depression, and suicidal thoughts, and are on this particular journey of unleashing your superpower, then your calling is to *fall*—to descend into the darkness of you to recover your sleeping deity (i.e., the hidden in the dark Goddess). Until the time that you journey into your *underworld* to reclaim all parts of you, you only operate at half capacity or only as half god. Activation is the reawakening of your hidden God consciousness from the dark, through the alchemical process of fire. In 2020, I produced a YouTube video titled, "**Pain Is Designed To Wake You Up Inside, So Are You Up Yet?**" It explores the realms of pain or being burned by the fires of pain, as necessary to jolt you out of deep psychological slumber. Meaning, if not for the pain that the fire brings, the discomfort it projects as mental disorder, your superpower remains dormant, hidden, and misused. It's easy for your power to be misused when you are asleep. It is as if your giant is sleeping, and anyone who's anyone has the chance to walk past and poke it without any rebuttal from you. How can you possibly respond when you are asleep? Others will disrespect you and will not flinch because you will not move. They've come by so many times to steal from you, destroy you, usurp from your power reserve, and you've done nothing. Why? Because your God-beast lies stuck in the darkness, and you remain asleep unable to awaken it until someone or something comes along with enough pain to shock your ass awake. Also known as, to awaken the beast or sleeping giant within.

> "A goddess is a woman who achieved the impossible, she befriended the beast inside of her. Her demons fight by her side. She is a divine paradox. She realized her darkness is full of light, she is an alchemist."— Unknown

Activate

In the previously channeled message it was said, "**You fear the dark because of the devil and demons that live there, when in fact they are YOU.**" Let's dive even deeper into this concept shall we? To do this, I have once again allowed for deeper channeling through my unlocked intuitive ancient wisdoms from higher and lower sources. I can only give it to you the way it is given to me.

> **Downloaded/Uploaded/ Intuitively Channeled Message**
>
> You embody that which you were told to fear, hide, and suppress; therefore, the disorder in your mind is the push and pull confusion between what you are and what you have been told you are. Instead of joining together both your God and Devil, Sun and Moon, Father God and Mother Goddess, you have been taught to pit these infinite forces against one another within you. Rather than doing the inner work to unify them, you have been led to only accept one part and fear the other, thus fearing yourself. They say new levels equals new devils, but what you don't know is that your new level also makes you a new devil. You are the new devil who will be highly feared by those who poked you when you were asleep. Not because you're evil, but because those that attempted to usurp from you, those who attempted to delay your awakening, missions, and divine purpose will seek to hide from your alchemized-risen fire when you show up fully integrated in all your powers. Why? Because they will know that you SEE them for all they truly are and are not. Your power will anger them because you will reflect the inner work they refuse to do in themselves. So, they will attempt to mock your abilities and slander your name by saying you are possessed, that you worship the devil and commune with demons, and they will be correct! Correct only in the knowing that the devil and demon to which they refer was the suppressed goddess hidden in the darkness of pain now exalted in her rightful power, as she always should have been.

> However, remember, the devil is also an angel too. Which makes you both god and devil, both angel and demon. Your concept of demons is out of order! Which in turn causes disorder in your mind and body. Demons are angels that live in the dark, so know this: It is the demons that live in the darkness of the people who refuse to do the inner-activation through divine alchemy to raise their fires up that seek to harm you (***read that again***). Not to fret, there will be those that have also done the inner work that will honor and protect you, as you will them, because you all will know and respect the journey you both took through hell, to rise into your own heaven on earth.
>
> ## —The All, The Light and Dark, Angel and Demon, God and Devil

"You would be surprised to know that the word devil and the word divine have the same roots; they come from the same roots. In Sanskrit divine is called Deva, from Deva comes the English word divine and the devils. In fact, the Devil and God are two sides of the same coin. There is neither God nor Devils, you are either asleep or awake."— **OSHO, Indian Mystic & Leader**

Your descent down into the darkness of your mind and emotions is the journey to reawakening your pseudo (***defined as: to mock, mislead, or assume***) devil, your SHE DEVIL. You never heard of anyone saying "he-devil", so by golly, the devil must be a woman, well at least according to our lovely 17th century witch and women hunters. Remember if you were naturally born with the qualities of ***intuition, clairvoyance, beauty, ancient knowledge and wisdom, foresight, sensuality and sexuality, charm, empathic abilities, fiery passion*** for those you love and the things you truly care about, and if you **speak out** and ***question the motives*** of anyone calling themselves leaders, you are a witch who gets her powers from the devil, Lucifer (perhaps take some time to do your own research on the derivatives of these names; it may open up an entirely new world for you). Well, in the case of re-ordering mental dis-order about who and what we are outside of the contradicting ideologies we have all been taught, I'd say these accusations are absolutely, a hundred percent plausible. Correct only in the sense that those of us born with DNA coded spiritual gifts receive our powers from not just a higher source, but also from lower source: Hence the phrases: **"As above so below; as within so without."** Meaning, you embody the characteristics of that which has lived in the darkness and is made up of the fires of hell, i.e., Your inner **Phoenix**.

Your inner hell (Phoenix) fire is there to do two very important things for the initiate who is called to activate and turn their pain into power.

- To burn away/consume everything you are not, and everything you thought you were.
- To refine everything that you truly are.

Have you ever heard of the phrase "raise hell"? Perhaps you've heard of it in the sense where someone said, "***You better stop that before she comes in here and raises hell.***" Where do you think this phrase came from? The misconception of this phrase loses its benevolence in the minds and hearts of those unequipped to decipher ancient wisdom. The idea of raising hell is synonymous to the activation of raising your inner fire, and the rising up of your Phoenix out of the shadows. To raise hell doesn't necessarily mean to cause chaos and havoc on all, quite the contrary! To those who've done and continue to do the inner dark-work required for wellbeing, this phrase suggests raising your Phoenix out of hell to burn away attachments to people, ideas, places, and things that have caused chaos, and disorder in your life, mind, and body. So, to this new philosophy on what it really means to raise hell for the activated ones, I say, "***We don't need no water let that mutha-fucka burn.***"

> ### Downloaded/Uploaded/ Intuitive Channeled Message
>
> When some realize that this journey is the activation of power as opposed to anxiety, wanting to die a physical death, and depression, others will pretend that they too are suppressing power, when in fact, they are the abusers of it. They will wear masks to appear that they are intuitive, they will wear masks as if they are empaths, they will wear masks as if they are clairvoyant—because they want to covet the warrior title of those divine ones that have taken the journey through darkness. Some may say that because they have gone through their ideas of hell that they have taken this particular journey to rise, but not so! As this journey is designed to set free those held captive, not those who seek to capture. They will come across as if they've gone through certain pains and have risen through to power; however, they instead would be the ones who attempt to compete and attack with this fire's power. They will attempt to usurp the divine gifts of those chosen to carry out specific missions by brute force of hate, competition, mockery, slander, and passive covert insults. There are many who avoid taking the journey through their true darkness to rise, and/or haven't been called to. They will come across as if they have done the inner-shadow work and will wear the mask of doing great work for the collective; however, this is not a display of mental disorder but of mental illness. You will know them by the energetic fruits they bear.
>
> ## —The All, The Ancestors

This isn't a journey anyone would want to pretend they've taken, because as I mentioned before, this fire does two things: it consumes all that is false and it refines all that is truly you. Meaning, if a person is wearing a mask of truth, but they indeed are false in and of themselves, then this fire will completely consume them—thus leaving behind the mask of truth. This fire is completely intelligent and can only commune (*communion: the sharing or exchanging of intimate thoughts and feelings, especially when the exchange is on a mental or spiritual level*) with that which is like itself; and anything that is not like it will be consumed or burned by it. As I write this portion, I am activating downloaded and uploaded information that wants to speak through me to you who is reading this book. As usual, I can only offer this ancient wisdom to you as it is given to me.

Downloaded/Uploaded/Channeled Message

Those who refuse to take the journey through the darkness of their mind and emotions to fully activate this power, this fire to raise it up for activation through their bodies to their higher mind and attempt to operate this fire power from their lower selves will be killing themselves. This fire will not consume and refine such as the process of alchemy, instead this fire will consume them completely. This power that is bubbling underneath the surface showing up as anxiety and depression (for those who have suppressed their abilities due to fear, slander, mockery, due to being hated and hated-on), has evolved in its intelligence. It's so intelligent that it will no longer operate for the person efficiently and effectively unless it is fully risen for activation through the alchemical process of turning pain into power. If anyone attempts to access this fire and power by any other means other than raising it up for activation, it will consume them completely, meaning it will destroy them from the inside out. Meaning the spreading of mental illness and disease (disease) in the body. Those who have attempted to misuse and abuse this power display the poisonous behaviors of "*hurt people, hurting people.*"

Because she has been misused and abused for so long, she is done with that! When others say that God never changes and stays the same, this is a lie. God is ever changing and shifting. God and Goddess live within each and every person, since this is the case, look at yourselves to see how much God continues to evolve.

This intelligent power (i.e., the suppressed divine feminine, the suppressed Goddess) has also evolved in what she will accept and will not accept to protect itself. She will no longer allow herself to be misused and abused. THIS IS GROWTH! Anyone who attempts to access this Goddess powers for misuse and abuse, will self-destruct from the inside out. The harm they attempt to send out will backfire—BACK-FIRE. The fire will in-fold back onto the source, the sender (the person), and consume them. You must do the inner work to not only attempt to access this power, but raise it up. You can no longer pretend to do this work, and it will be obvious to decipher who has done this work, because they will be the ones that will not need to compete with others. Power that is fully risen in and of itself, TRUE POWER, intelligently knows that trying to compete with another is competing with itself, thus harming itself. You will know risen power because it is not intimidated by anyone else (man or woman) in their power. It will not hate or seek to hate-on anyone else in their power, because it knows that this would be self-sabotaging. As a matter of fact, this power encourages others to rise, because it knows that it is merely expanding itself by doing so. It sees a reflection of itself in others in their power and is proud and happy to be a part of that. Why would anyone or anything seek to harm its own reflection?

— The Divine Feminine, The Ancient Ones, The Ancestors

"People will do anything, no matter how absurd, in order to avoid facing their own Soul. One doesn't become enlightened by imagining figures of light, but by making the darkness conscious." Carl Jung

Activate

The journey into the darkness of your mind and emotions is a quest, for those of you who are called to gain your mental and emotional health through the revelation of hidden in the dark truths about who and what you are, outside of everything you've ever been taught. Only to rise again having burned away all that is not you, as the Phoenix through the fire—from the ashes of the old false beliefs systems and ideas.

In the following chapters, I'll talk more about what my personal journey looked like as I answered the call to descend down into my inner hell darkness, but for now I want to share something with you. As I began to do the inner shadow work to uncover why anxiety, depression, and suicidal thoughts showed up for me, my dreams, visions, and synchronicities INCREASED exponentially. So much in fact, that I would be led to wake up in the wee hours of the morning to write them or voice-record them. Because often if you wait too long to transcribe them, you realize you will have forgotten them come sunrise; thus, missing out on the imperative messages your spiritual guides and ancestors are trying to tell you.

The following is one of the first of many images I saw during my sleeping astral-dream states. It reflects not only the proof that I had descended down into my underworld, but that I indeed had accessed my hidden shadow.

Visual sketch by Timmésha Burgess, representing the ascent of her shadow-self, powers, and hidden gifts to the surface.

In my dream state of astral travels, I witnessed myself flying upward in a pitch-black darkness, the dark image you see in my sketch is really my attempt to draw a shadow. What I really saw was a shadow of myself (the image above) reflecting against a wall. I was only able to tell it was my shadow because there was a flash of lightning (literally one bolt that flashed once) that lit up the space, and only then was I able to see my shadow reflected. I could hear the sound of my massive wings flapping as I ascended upward. As I flew upward, my experience shifted me into the cosmos. I say cosmos because I was above the earth's atmosphere and coming floating toward me were several large multi-colored crystals.

In my sketch above take notice of the written portions that read the following:

- Thunder and lightning in my astral
- Saw my shadow from the lightning I was taking flight with my own wings
- Rainbow crystals
- Hidden talents/remembering

These writings were intuitively downloaded to me as channeled messages that were clarifying for me, that I indeed had taken the journey to uncover what was hidden in the darkness of me. By this time I had this astral dream, I was well prepared to understand, innerstand, and overstand its symbolism as it related to my inner work to remember and unleash my born-with-it gifts that were held captive within me. Taking into the above explanation of the idea of hell and hell fire, I am now receiving clarity on the concept of "**Flying like a bat out of hell**," and I laugh hysterically!

As I began to write this portion of this book, I asked for guidance from all of my spirit guides, my higher and lower selves. I even decided to ask *Carl Jung* if he would be so kind as to train me as his student. I Googled a photo of Carl and placed him on my altar for a few nights. I introduced him to my grandparents (their pictures are also affixed on my altar), and to others I deem as my guides in the spiritual realms. As I stared at his photos, I said, "*Hey Carl, I'm being guided to birth this book and I know I can't do it alone, at least not without supernatural help. Your philosophies were life-saving for me when I was called and decided to answer the call to take the dark journey. Will you guide me on my writings? Please feel free to teach and visit me in my dreams and visions because I am a dreamer and visionary.*" And exactly two nights later, I dreamt of the following experience and image below.

This experience revealed to me that my astral dream was my alchemical process of initiation. In my experience, my consciousness spun down rapidly—so fast in fact, that I became almost nauseated by the speed. Then suddenly, my consciousness reversed its spin and began spinning back up. In the following sketch, you'll notice how I did my best to draw what I experienced. On my way up, I saw a woman dark as dark as night, like a charcoal-colored being with glowing green eyes looking at me through the spin of my consciousness spinning upward. It wasn't until a few days later that I decided to draw my experience why? Because within days, I was intuitively led to pull up Carl Jung lectures on alchemy and psychology, and low-and-behold I came across a video on Jung Monterey's YouTube channel titled, "**Jung, Alchemy, and the Tree of Life— Eva Rider**." Eva presented multiple photos that depicted their greatest examples of this alchemical process, and among those examples was a photo called, "The spiral."

I screamed, and danced, and laughed in my living room— damn near knocking over everything, because this was it! I knew that what I experienced was my final (yet not final) step in activating my inner alchemist to transform my existence, my life, and my world FOREVER. I paused the video for a moment, rewound it a few times and shook my head at the sheer fact that this shit is NO JOKE, and that I along with so many others, and those to come have been initiated into ancient wisdom and power. Wisdoms and powers that for too long had been monopolized by those who sought to overpower, overrule, and overthrow the balance of all.

Later that night and for the next three nights, I took my time to draw what my initiation looked like and the dark being I saw. As I started to sketch, my inner ancient self said, "***Damn, she's me—The shadow me—The hidden in the dark divine feminine***"!

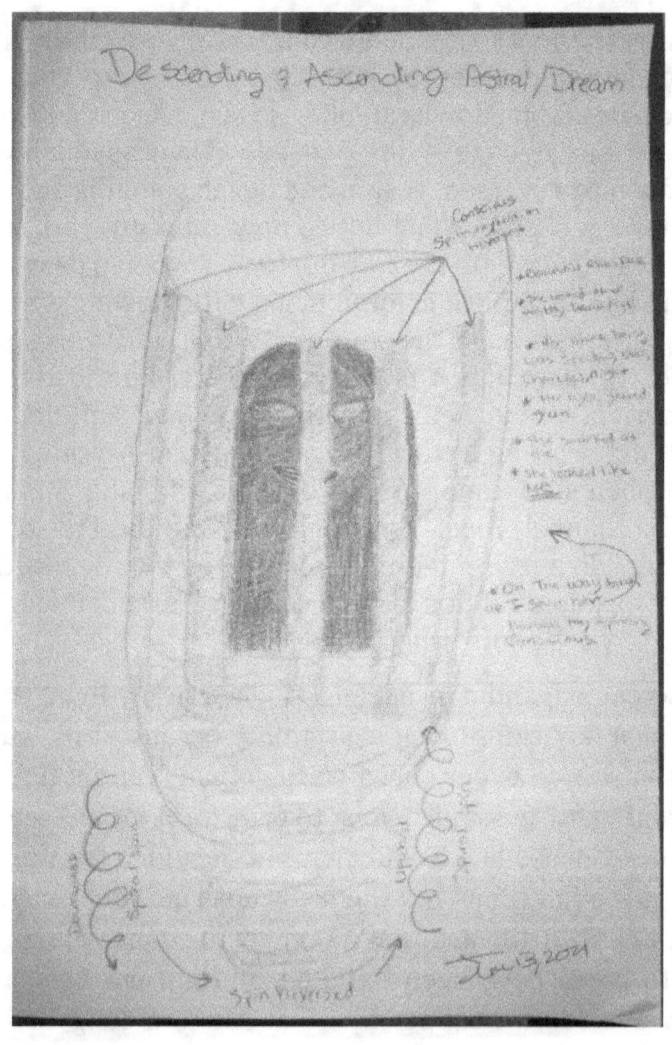

Descending and Ascending Consciousness Sketch by Timmésha Burgess

In my sketch you will notice the following wording from left to right, and upward;

- Downward spiral/spin.
- Spin reversed.
- Upward spiral/spin
- On my way back up I saw her through my spinning conscious.
- She looked like me.
- She smirked at me.
- Her eyes glowed green (Representing that she is led from her heart space. Heart chakra represented by the color green.).
- Her entire being was shadow, black, charcoal, night.
- She looked other-worldly, beautiful (despite my unskilled sketch hand).
- Beautiful alien-like.
- Conscious spinning/motion movement (the bars represent spinning as if looking through an old rotating film).

If you or someone you know has had dreams and/or visions similar to my sketch, then nine times out of ten, they scared the shit out of you. They scared you only in the fact that there was no one around to interpret for you what seeing an image like this even symbolizes for the person experiencing it.

- Can you imagine drawing an image like this in the 16th or 17th century and it getting out to the public?
- Can you imagine the detrimental effects it would have on the psyche of the woman, man, or child who drew images like this from their dreams only to be accused of being evil or wicked. Which evil spelled backward is live—live

is also defined as *connected to a source of electric current. synonyms: electrified, charged, powered, connected, active, having life.*

Taking into consideration the last bullet, one could suggest that this particular journey of uncovering the hidden superpower bubbling underneath the surface of their anxiety, depression, and suicidal ideations has more to do with the connection to something much more powerful, alive, charged, active, and sentient (***able to perceive or feel things.: conscious, aware***).

So, earlier I mentioned that I'd provide insight into what it looked like for me on my journey, when I began to descend into my inner darkness. Again, as mentioned at the beginning of this chapter, I like to look at the journey through the darkness of mental and emotional health as a three-part alchemical journey. A journey through alchemical phases in which I call **Twilight**, **Dusk**, and **Dawn**.

The *twilight*, *dusk*, and *dawn* phases are exactly where I found myself on my journey through the darkness of my mind, so much so that I was psychically led to give each phase a title. Titles that would signify that surely there was a way in, but that there was always a way through and ultimately . . . out! These phases are the points of *initiation* in which you journey down into the great darkness (i.e., your inner hell) to ***first*** **UNLEASH** and ***second*** **ACTIVATE** your suppressed superpower (i.e., phoenix) for mental and emotional health. In the following sections, I will:

1. Dive deep into each *initiation* phase down into the darkness of your mind and body (***Twilight***).
2. Share what I was called to do, undo, learn, and unlearn on my personal journey through my inner hell (***Dusk***).

3. Provide insight on the necessary inner work required to unleash, and raise fire for full activation of all of your body centers and higher mind for mental and emotional stability (*Dawn*).

Activate

TWILIGHT.

The *transitional phase*. A period or state of obscurity, ambiguity, or gradual decline. An uncertain, gloomy, and terminal period of gradual decline.

In the Twilight alchemical phase you will go through the following:

1. Question absolutely everything about yourself, your decisions, and the world in which you live and in which you've built your life.

2. Realize that you have spent most of your life trying to find your purpose and reason for being born, only to discover it right there, showing up as mental health disorders. OH, THE IRONY!

When twilight began for me, I was at a place in my life when I was ready and willing to question absolutely everything! But keep in mind that phases can last for years depending on where you are or where you are not, because as the saying goes, "When the student is ready, the teacher will appear." During this time in my life I was in and out of relationships and doing pretty well financially as I was successfully running my own consulting company, but I felt like I was on a hamster wheel. A wheel of a series of disappointing relationships and average life. My twilight lasted approximately two years, showing up first as confusion about who I was and why I was even alive at all. At this time, I ceased going to church, I stopped groveling in prayers and started asking some bold questions out loud to the sky when no one was around. Questions like, **"What is this all for anyway?"** For months, I listened to all things Abraham Hicks, and was drawn to different teachings on the universe and the cosmos. One day I was driving along and was accosted by a male driving in an SUV next to me. I can remember it so well, because on this particular day I was in an all-time low mood. I remember feeling like I wanted to cry while I was driving, and even thought to pull over so I could. Nothing in particular happened that day that made me feel sad, but I did! I mean, a deep, intense kind of grief as if someone had died. That someone was me, although I didn't know it yet. For the next week or so I started to get to know this fella that I met in the car next to me. One day he called to ask me if I wanted to have lunch. I happened to be heading on a hike at the time and invited him to come along. Instead of going for food he met me at one of my frequent hiking spots. As we walked, I remember our conversation went from simple comments about the events of our week to all things the vortex and the cosmos. I remember saying to him, "I find myself searching for answers I can't find on Google." He turned to me and said, "I will do my best (Bes) to help you. Sometime later, I found that my new acquaintance had earned his stripes as a 33rd degree Mason, and within him was a reservoir of all the answers I had been seeking. I mentioned *Bes* in parenthesis above; I did this because in some conversations later with this Mason, he mentioned that he didn't say that he'd do his "best" to help me, but that he'd do his "Bes" to help me. He later explained that Bes was an ancient Egyptian god, whom together with his feminine counterpart Beset, was worshipped as a protector of households and, in particular, of mothers, children, and childbirth. Bes later came to be regarded as the defender of everything good and the enemy of all that is bad. Now he had not mentioned that he was a Mason initially. If he had, I wouldn't have even known what that meant really, at least not concerning me and my life. But what I uncovered a couple of years later as I was watching a YouTube video by **Sevan Bomar** titled, *Goddess and the Explorer*, was that the role of any Mason is to awaken the sleeping **Divine Feminine**. Mission accomplished!

As I recited the famous quote earlier, **when the student is ready, the teacher will appear**, and this was the precipice of my twilight. When I started to ask the hard questions about life, creation, God, and everything else, this being/teacher appeared just in the nick of time and just when I needed it most! My crossing paths with this teacher was nothing short of divine intervention, sending the right person at the right time to water the seeds of ancient wisdom that were buried DEEP within my subconscious and DNA. To him and to the many teachers that shed light into the darkness for me who may not even know they have, I am forever grateful.

This teacher and I later began cultivating a romantic union, one that ended shortly after it began for a few reasons. But what I *understood*, *overstood*, and *innerstood* as I began to go deeper into my inner world was that he was only sent as a guide. He was a man, just a being in his flesh who struggled with his own inner darkness, and I was NEVER meant to date him, but to learn from him. One of the deepest lessons I learned was that many of us get it wrong when we meet someone of the opposite sex. It's as if our minds have been trained to a default setting of automatically sizing someone up for a relationship just because they have approached us in a healthy way. Earlier, when I mentioned that I was in and out of relationships, this would only make sense due to the fact that I was on a path where almost everyone and everything I allowed around me would HAVE to cease to exist on my path in more ways than one. This is proof that I was entering a point in my life where everyone and everything that was out of alignment with what I was becoming and unbecoming HAD TO GO!

At this twilight juncture in my life, I started to fully adopt the practices of meditation. Why? Because, I needed to sit with all the insight that I was learning from my Masonic teacher sent to me by the universe. As a matter of fact, we cultivated an even exchange as it related to sharing insight. I assisted him with and through meditative practices, and he shared his learned ancient teachings with me. By doing this, I was able to get to the core of when and where I learned to hide and disguise whatever was ready to break free from me. I allowed my inner world to have its way and take me on an inner journey into realms I had never been taught to explore. My mind went back to not just the beginning of my right life, but it went backward and forward to many beginnings! Flashes and images of me in places I had never been (not in this lifetime) would enter my mind: mountains, desert lands, lush green forests, and large colosseum like structures. I would see my feet walking lands, lush pastures alongside wild animals that all seemed to be a part of the kingdom that I inhabited. And when I slept at night, I'd have dreams and enter parallel universes where I'd see myself as a completely black (black as asphalt) being, standing 20 feet tall, with green glowing eyes, and locked hair down to my waist.

I started opening myself up to communicating with my ancestors, and asking my grandparents who had transcended years ago, what I was seeing, and why I was seeing these things? What later came to me was that these visions were flashes of past lives I had lived, now coming to the surface as I took the journey through the richness of my mind. The reason they were coming to the surface was because it was time to dive deeper into the core of not only who, but *what* I really was underneath the surface of what I looked like to the outside world and to myself in the mirror.

Activate

Dusk

(Dusk—complete darkness). The phase where you learn to see in the dark, and when you feel you cannot see, this is where you MUST learn to *feel* your way through. But remember, it is always *darkest before the dawn*. This is the point where you enter your idea of hell, and where death (transition) happens in more ways than one.

In the Dusk alchemical phase you will likely:

1. Feel like you are losing your mind, or are going crazy.
2. Become dissatisfied with your current profession/job or work environment.
3. Quit or be terminated from place of employment.
4. Question your beliefs and what you've been taught by society, family structures, and religion.
5. Feel an increase of anxiety, depression, suicidal ideations, and panic attacks.
6. Face hard and painful truths about those you've called your friends and family members.
7. Contemplate or attempt suicide.
8. Become paranoid.
9. Breakup with your boyfriend/girlfriend/spouse/partner.
10. Be drawn to tarot cards/readings.
11. Be drawn to the cosmos.

12. Talk to yourself.
13. Notice synchronicities and symbols everywhere daily (billboards, clocks, license plates, movies, social media, animals, music, etc.).
14. Experience insomnia.
15. Isolate from former acquaintances, certain family members, and social circles.

I was completely exhausted mentally, emotionally, physically, and FINANCIALLY from fighting for my mother's freedom and maintaining a level head in my own day-to-day personal and work life. I had nothing else to offer the world or anyone. The little that I did have left was hope. But after a while, even hope faded, and all that was left was me, sitting in a dark room, candles lit all around me, tears running down my face soaking the carpet beneath me, screaming out to anything in the heavens and on earth that would listen to me saying, "***HELP ME! I FEEL LIKE I'M LOSING A BATTLE I DIDN'T EVEN KNOW I WAS IN. I DON'T KNOW WHAT'S HAPPENING OR WHERE TO GO FROM HERE!***"

The response I received back after crying out was a series of startling truths both seen and hidden, revelations that struck me to my core. I could feel the energy in my living room shift from slightly warm to cold, but my body remained extremely hot to the point I was sweating. I lay stretched out on my living room floor, my arms spread out on either side, my eyes closed, and all I could internally hear was, *"Oh you don't know where to go from here? You don't know who you are, what to do or what to say?! Then go into the dark!"*

My spiritual, unseen, and ancestor guides made it clear to me that I was on a much more divinely guided path through darkness that many did not and could not survive for many reasons. Why? Because this journey isn't for the faint of heart but a hellish path designed to equip those chosen to carry out specific missions throughout their lives. It's the road less traveled, most hated, and most feared. **Hence**, why those who are called on this path are hated, feared, and isolated. It was made clear to me that I wasn't just going through darkness in my life, but that the dark times in my day to day were the destruction of all things not aligned with my divine *power, mission*, and *life's purpose*. At several points during my journey through my inner dark world, I felt that I couldn't continue, that I couldn't learn one more hard lesson or face another debilitating truth about all the shit I had once accepted and called normal.

While in this phase of my life, things were crashing all around me, and I found myself having to quit my consulting work and leave my clients because of attacks from women on the job. Romantic affiliations ended abruptly due to serious offenses and betrayals like when one guy slept with a friend-girl of mine and another threatened to kill me and my entire family because I refused to continue seeing him. In this phase, I found out that some women I called friends from childhood had slandered my name and my family's name when my mother was sent to prison, and that men and women that I adopted as friends later became enemies who sabotaged business opportunities for me behind closed doors due to envy and jealousy. I mean, you name it, and I was more than likely experiencing the shit in my darkness.

During my dark phase;

- My mother was wrongfully sentenced to twenty years in prison.
- I found out that a group of people conspired to sabotage my business and opportunities to further expand into the tech and special-needs space.

- People stole and took credit for my consulting work through my company Synergy (Plus+) which before was Burgess Association for DDPs. They attempted to steal my creative ideas regarding Fireside Chats for Global Women (people I thought I could trust, called to get insight into what I was doing, then went off to duplicate it on their platforms).
- I was physically assaulted at work.
- People conspired to steal money from me **repeatedly.**
- Spell work (alchemy) was done to not only block my opportunity for elevation but to also attempt to kill me **repeatedly.**
- My skin was breaking out chronically.
- I became unemployed due to being blacklisted in the special-needs compliance consulting space.
- Had to apply for unemployment and receive food stamps ... again (once in college then again in my early to mid 20s).
- Became unable to continue to pay any of my bills. When I began to descend downward into my inner darkness, my middle sister Jessica was beginning to shift and evolve in her own personal life. It just so happened that she had decided to relocate from Miami to Georgia to start anew. She moved in with me at the beginning of my fall *(i.e., my journey downward)*, and I remember saying to her a few times when I'd get home from working late, **"Hey sis... I feel a change coming. I don't know how much longer I'm gonna last. Will you be able to handle it, the bills and things soon because I don't know what's going to happen. I'm tapped completely out in every way?"** She would always say, **"I got us, sis, don't worry."** If it weren't

for Jessica and the universe aligning our worlds at the perfectly appointed time ... *you fill in the blank.*)

- Lived off my savings and used them to pay for attorney fees to fight for my mother's freedom.
- Was abandoned by most people I called friends and family.
- Was abandoned by the attorney (second attorney) who stopped answering phone calls and emails once he received payment
- And to top it all off, a former friend of the family called me one day to say, "***Criminals ... y'all ain't nothing but a bunch of criminals!***" I imagined that because I also had two siblings that had had their run-ins with the law, that to him we were a bunch of good-for-nothings. **Truth moment, though:** I allowed whatever fire was brewing underneath me that I had been holding onto unleash without giving any thought to being polite. ALL BETS WERE OFF on being polite when it came to basic respect for me and *mi familia*. I cursed his ass out from here to kingdom come! He hung up the phone on me before I could get to my final blow, because I was going to *Mortal Kombat* his ass and "**FINISH HIM**"! I suppose my higher self and all of my ancestors gathered around me at that moment to bring me comfort; because I had lost full control... all I saw was the color red.
- I was literally, broke, broken, broken-hearted, and broken out!

I share all of this in a nutshell because it's imperative that you know who, what, when, and how forces may show up while you're in the dark. When you decide to start asking the universe, God, angels, or whomever or whatever who you are and why you were born at all, expect all hell to break loose within you and all around you! **But please note, that hell can be an exciting place once you learn through the guidance of your spiritual team that dwells in the dark how to journey through it.** As I traveled deeper within my hell, my outer world also began to crumble in every way imaginable and unimaginable. I realized that the destruction of people, places, and things were reflections of an out-of-power life I had lived and called normal; that would cease to exist evermore for me. As we know, anything that is built on an unsteady foundation—whether it be mentally, physically, and spiritually—is doomed to not only fail but crash and burn in such a way that there can be NO POINT of return. That's actually the goal, TO NEVER RETURN! I was embarking into a new place within, a place where I was completely alone, in the dark, afraid, but I refused to turn back!

In my darkness I *understood*, *overstood*, and *innerstood* that with the experience of an absent father, sexual abuse, and betrayals by those close to me; anxiety and depression grew stronger in the presence of certain people, places and things. When I would be in the presence of certain people, doing certain things, or in certain places, immediately my body reacted as if to communicate that a perceived or imminent danger was present. Anxiety began to act as some sort of alert mechanism that suggested to me I should attempt to escape—not because I was afraid of the people, but because of who I felt I would have to become to defend and protect myself from them. I realized that on my list of all the things I may have feared, I forgot to put myself.

Afraid of who I felt I would have to become in order to defend and protect myself—even now this idea arouses me to the core. Why? Because I had never been introduced to this part of me that had the capacity to defend and protect itself to this degree. This part of me was much braver than the me I had always known; this part of me felt like fire burning in my womb. It scared me to think of what this me was capable of if she ever was fully unleashed. In this darkness, I was introduced to this fiery me that I had kept hidden in the dark due to the fear of what she was capable of. This me didn't feel at all petty, competitive, or overly sensitive, NOT AT ALL, but it was intelligent enough to defend herself in ways that were tribal in a sense. Meaning, she was **ready, willing**, and **skilled** at wielding a sword and cutting the heads off of any mutha-fucka if it meant life or death for her and those she loved.

This hidden-in-the-dark me wanted revenge, wanted all of those who came for her and wrongfully attacked her to suffer miserably. This hidden-in-the-dark me would often sit back and imagine snatching out the tracheas of my enemies and listening to them gargle and choke to death on their own blood. This hidden-in-the-dark me wanted to pull the bodies of my attackers through a small hole and watch their flesh peel from their bodies. And this hidden me wanted a throne made out of the skin of all my enemies who wrongfully attacked and attempted to kill me.

Truth Moment: I have tortured and killed certain people who seriously attempted to kill, steal, and destroy me without cause other than their own jealousy and hate; over and over and over and over again . . . in my head! At times I'd laugh at myself when I'd see a person who attempted to bring me harm, because when I'd see them I'd say to myself, "***This fucker doesn't even know that I chopped their ass up into little, tiny pieces last night.***"

Are you side-eyeing this part of **Activate** yet? If you are, then you may not yet be on this particular journey of uncovering why anxiety, depression, and suicidal ideations have shown up for you. Because to journey into the darkness of our mind and emotions means no longer shoving down these deep, dark, hidden other truths about how pissed off, sad, and angry we get in times of pain, backstabbing, and undeserving betrayals. This journey into your inner hell isn't about putting on yet another mask of Pollyanna but about facing your dark nature. Your darkest, most hidden, and scary truths that you vowed to never unleash or reveal . . . not even to yourself. My journey through the darkness of my mind and body, aka my inner hell, forced me to reveal myself to myself, to have a conversation and forge a relationship with the demons I and so many have been taught to keep silent, hidden, disguised, and covered up. For the first time in my life (or shall I say this life), I was coming into *divine union* with what we call the Devil, aka my inner **Savage.**

Now, before I continue this descent down into our inner hells to connect to the devil or Savage, I MUST reiterate again that this particular journey is for those who are challenged by mental disorders such as anxiety, depression, and suicidal ideation due to the suppression of their superpower. In previous chapters, I delved deep into the categorical differences between *mental disorder* and *mental illness*. Remember that according to this particular body of work and new-age philosophy on mental disorder, those who perpetually seek to kill, steal, and destroy due to jealousy, hate, and their desire to compete and sabotage others suffer from mental illness NOT mental disorders. Therefore, when you notice anyone displaying these harmful characteristics, then you will know that they have *purposely* decided to unleash their inner Savage to start ridiculous and unnecessary wars, NOT end them.

You will know the difference between the two based on the characteristics and energy they display. You won't be able to be fooled because based on their energy, you will be able to tell if they have done the inner dark-work to raise their Savage through the process of alchemical activation. Even if they *appear* aesthetically beautiful on the surface and attempt to wear masks of love and care, you will be able to detect their falsehood from lightyears away. When you have taken this journey into the darkness to fully activate, you will not be able to be deceived by those who wear the masks of love publicly, but devise deceitful matters privately. How? Because you will know yourself, and knowledge of self allows you to see yourself or lack thereof in others. Also, your inner lower-self (aka demon/dark angel) and higher self (aka light angel), through your work to integrate the two, will always reveal the truth of anyone and anything through intuitive sparks, visions, dreams, and vibes. This dark journey trains you to **listen to what's not being said, to read in between the lines of all that is said and done, and to feel into the energy of all that is seen and unseen**. If you need a reminder on the differences between those that hunt/haunt for power (mental illness) and those that are hunted/haunted for their power (mental disorder), scroll back to chapters one and three and read the channeled, downloaded, and uploaded messages written in red letters.

So, my journey through the darkness of my mind and body, aka my inner hell, forced me to reveal myself to myself, to have a conversation and forge a relationship with the demons, the savage that I was taught to silence, hide, disguise, and cover up. This Savage was the one I hid in the shadows that began to show up as anxiety, depression, and suicidal thoughts. Remember earlier when I mentioned that anxiety would seem to flare up when I was around certain people, places, and things? Well, on this particular journey I found that what I thought was anxiety for me was really this inner Savage wanting to come up to the surface to defend me—and for good reason!

For example, some of the people I used to congregate around proved themselves to be untrustworthy, conniving, secretly competitive, and deceitful. I'd cross paths with women and men who would approach me to do business, only to find out they were using my ideas, taking them back as their own, all the while telling others not to do business with me as they brought my ideas to tables and rooms as their own. There were women that befriended me privately and slandered me publicly—yes, I said that right. On weekends, they were at my home, eating my cooked food, spending the night, crying on my shoulders, hanging around me and my family, and would even invite me out saying, "Hey girl let's do lunch," but in public and professional spaces, they'd act like they hardly even knew me.

I remember one day having a conversation with a colleague who weeks prior said to me, "***You're really good as a DDP, I can take you traveling with me to do more work***." It was said in the presence of my client and her staff members, and they all responded with ***ohhhs*** and ***ahhhhs***, as if it was an honor to be told that by this particular person. Well, about one year later, after my client hired the young lady that attempted to fight me (mentioned in chapter one), she later responded, "***Girl, you can't handle me***," while shooing her hand at me after I asked her about working more closely together. She did this in front of the same group of people as before, except with the new addition of the one that was out for my job title and pay. They all smirked at one another and scoffed. I mentioned to her how much of a change there had been in her response from just a year prior, and I looked over at the rest of everyone's faces and knew at that moment . . . that a shift happened. It wasn't because my work went from good to bad, quite the contrary, my name and company were gaining a highly sought-after reputation for great work. So much so, that one of the major auditing agencies named Delmarva at the time, made mention of my great work as a consultant to my clients and the state. So my work game was strong, but there was something else; a presence and energy in the air that was out for blood . . . my blood. I later found out that this same woman (who also happened to be the woman that recommended this client to me) was secretly competitive. As I began to grow my business and ascend in the profession of compliance, my name and company name had reached the state level due to my skills and how damn good I was at my job. However, through the process of ascending in my business, those that I gathered around taught me that I was allowed to be good, but not as good, as thorough, or better than them.

So when I said that anxiety for me was really this inner Savage wanting to come up to the surface to defend me around certain people, places, and things—this is what I mean. When *certain* circumstances arose in my day to day, professional and personal life she (the savage) was the one raising her head up through the expression of anxiety, like a snake (kundalini) ready to strike as if to say, "***Tag me in!***" She was the one that would shed light on the apparent bullshit, hate, fuckery, and sabotage. She was and is the one, for so many on this particular journey, that needs to be rescued from the shadows. Anxiety and depression for many of us who have been hunted/haunted on this particular journey of unleashing and activating our suppressed superpower, are the sirens of our most Savage feminine goddess saying, "***Ohhhhh, please tag me in!***"

However, we've taught ourselves to vilify, shun, and hide her due to trying to save-face (sort of speak) or masking her under "overly" humble roles in hopes that those that hate us would turn to love us. Well, I've got a newsflash for you, their hate for you is by choice, and there isn't anything you can do or even SHOULD do to attempt to earn love and respect. Why? Because on this journey through the darkness you learn to no longer seek to appease anyone who is hell-bent (*i.e., bent down into their hell and staying there on purpose, firm about it, single-minded, obsessive, fanatical, fixated*) on killing you, stealing from you, and destroying you based on their own desire for chaos.

You learn that the natural order and natural law of things on this planet and in this dimension are bound by the law of yin and yang, darkness and light, hate and love. You *understand, overstand,* and *innerstand* that there would be no balance of "the all" without it, meaning hate also has its place and belongs.

Timmesha Burgess

When you accept that hate just like love must both exist in the balance of life; you quickly *unlearn* the useless skill of people pleasing, and began to develop, adopt, and live by a new **Activated** philosophy that says the following:

> "**The journey through the darkness of mental health equips you with the *emotional intelligence* to no longer people-please. You learn not to question rather or not certain people like you, because if you have to question it then the answer is already clear. Instead, you evaluate if you even like them, and can trust them around your superpower.**"

What came to me when these things started to reveal themselves was a sudden epiphany—one so eye-opening that I took to social media (as I did with a lot of my deep philosophical insights) to share it with the public.

Social Media Post made August 2020. Phoenix Rising Exclusives was a short series, I've since retired it and re-branded all philosophy's for Fireside Chats for Global Women and within this written body of work of Activate.

Activate

In this darkness, I questioned not only everything about myself but the presence of every person in my life, including family members. Why? Because this journey through my inner darkness revealed that most of those that were closest to me always seemed to be present every time I experienced deep pains and betrayals and not as support systems. When I looked up to see who stabbed me and where yet another gushing wound came from, I always saw familiar faces.

The questions on my journey through the darkness of my mind and body then became as follows:

1. Why am I consistently congregating around people, places, and things I feel I need to defend and protect myself from?

2. Why am I nurturing what I should be neutering and neutering when I could be nurturing?

3. What is it about me that caused almost *every single person* in my life to hate, hate on, compete with, or attempt to sabotage me in the most vicious, unusually cruel and intentional ways?

So again, **the Savage or devil**, is the one that I and so many others have taught ourselves to suppress, mask, and hide in the dark under the guise is this not so? Isn't the devil described as a bad, evil entity and ruler of the underworld of hell? While there may be many definitions based on religious ideology about this pseudo term; one thing's for sure and that is we all as humans have been taught the same damn thing--- to accept one part of existence and reject another, yet we wonder why there is disorder; a split in our mind and body. What I've uncovered through the dusk phase was my own rejection of self; a dark natured self that like anything else deserved to be understood, innerstood, and overstood on my own. I realized that throughout my life, I hid this inner Savage under the auspices of

"*I know he/she didn't mean to insult me*", and "*I'm just being too sensitive or too emotional.*" How many times in your life have you pushed back in the desire to set fire to the rain when you had the chance to? Probably more than you can count! But here's the thing, we did the right thing pushing it back in even though we were subjecting ourselves to depression. Because until we have taken this particular journey through the dark to gain and refine emotional intelligence, and to raise our hell, devil, demons for alchemical activation, we would literally set the world on fire. The problem throughout centuries has been that NO ONE, NO ONE was emotionally intelligent enough to explore and teach from the place of ancient wisdom that says, YOU ARE BOTH God and the Devil, and why not? Because very few were willing to take the journey through their own inner darkness themselves. Instead, many offset their fear and ignorance of themselves onto others.

Now let's explore this concept of emotional intelligence that is gained and *refined* on the journey through the darkness. **Emotional intelligence** is defined as the capacity to be aware of, control, and express one's emotions and to handle interpersonal relationships judiciously and empathetically. Emotional intelligence is the key to both personal and professional success. Emotional intelligence is the alchemical vehicle required to raise up our hell fires for activation. The idea of emotional intelligence has been the *missing golden key* on how to properly train your dragon and work alongside your inner Savage, once you've accessed it.

To offer deeper insight into this concept of emotional intelligence as the golden key to raising your inner demon, devil, hell fires up for activation, I will allow my intuitive guides to further clarify. As usual, I can only share the message with you as it activated within me from my ancient sources.

Uploaded/Downloaded/Intuitively Channeled Message

You have taught yourselves and have been taught to suppress your Savage (aka inner demon, devil), because there was no one around to guide on the philosophy of emotional intelligence who was wise enough to share the ancient principles of this power. Your world of human beings were taught to fear what was not fully **understood**, **innerstood**, and **overstood**, thus shunning your power off as "that which (witch) must never be named" as nothing other than evil. This has been to your own detriment, thus perpetuating your own mental and emotional instability as a generational curse. To gain your mental health and refine your emotional intelligence through activation, you must come into power with the following:

1. Dismember and remember the word Evil for yourself. **Ev** = Eve, who supposedly ate the fruit of knowledge. **Vil** is short for vilify. The word evil taught you to condemn the concept of Eve, the feminine. If there was an Eve who ate the fruit, good for her! However, the story taught you to denounce her "the she in yourself" for asking, seeking, reading, being intelligent, and wise.

2. It makes complete sense why most of your world adopted the idea of fear relating to this power, because there were many that, as mentioned before, chose to unleash their dragon/Savage without having done the inner work on themselves to gain wisdom, emotional intelligence, and mental health.

3. There were many mentally ill ones that *knowingly* chose to unleash their dragon to harm instead of protect, and to kill instead of heal—those that misused and abused their dragon fire to overpower others and devise deceitful plans to rule the earth and everything and everyone on it. However, in this new age that has dawned on your planet, NO ONE will be able to access dragon

fire (Phoenix) at all unless they are an energetic match to do so. Your hidden in the dark power, your dark Goddess, has evolved in her intelligence and will not allow herself to be accessed nor unleashed unless the inner work of alchemical activation is done.

4. You have been misguided about your inner demon as one that if accessed, will only cause harm. This is true only in the case of those that did not do the inner work to raise their demon up for activation into their higher crowned center. Your anxiety, depression, and suicidal thoughts increase because you continue to shun and mask your inner demon in the dark instead of raising it up to be crowned. It is quite unfair and sad to infinite creation.

5. This power has been unfairly judged due to the unhealthy ego and poisonous minds (mental illness) of men and women who purposely misused and abused it ignorantly and selfishly. Darkness has never been bad. It has been humans' unhealthy ego that divided dark from light. Humans' unhealthy egos threw the rock, placed their hands behind their backs, and pointed the finger at the shadow saying, "**The darkness did it**." It was and is humans' unhealthy egos and lack of activation that separated you from your power. Such as the separation of God from Devil, angel from demon. They are and forever will be infinite parts of the *same whole*, joined together in divine union forever and ever. Your attempt to continue to tear them apart is the tearing apart and destruction of yourself. The tearing apart of darkness from the light, man from woman, and angel from demon. This is why disorder has shown up in your mind and emotions.

6. The issue is that you have not learned how to properly activate your inner hell fire, demon, devil, dark Goddess into full integration to rule alongside and with your inner heaven, angel, god, and light.

7. Many have set the incorrect examples of what demons and devils are. Remember, your human race has given this power such a derogatory name that when you hear the words demon, devil, or hell, you shrink, frown, and are ready to draw your

swords, merely because of a name. This is no fault of yours because you have witnessed and were victims of those that used their inner demons, dragons, and devils to cause nearly irreparable harm on you and others. But rest assured that this will no longer be able to occur, as this power has now evolved its intelligence concerning your existence, and therefore can no longer be accessed by those who refuse to do the inner work for mental and emotional health.

8. When you have descended into and through the darkness of your mind and emotions to access this bubbling underneath the surface fire power (superpower), you will have no place to go but UP. As you do the inner work by raising your power through the process of alchemical activation, you will then and only then be able to unleash this power. The unleashing can only happen because you have done the work to integrate both your God and Devil, your angel and demon.

9. When you feel the rise of anxiety, it is your inner Savage that you have suppressed banging at your locked doors within, that wants to be *included* in all that you do. Together your inner Savage (demon/devil) and God/Goddess will protect, guide, support, and love you. However, you have disregarded her, therefore she bubbles underneath the surface; now showing up as what you all call "anxiety."

10. DO NOT make the mistake many of your kind have already made by trying to unleash this suppressed superpower straight away without having done the work to raise it for activation, or else you will not only harm others, but you will harm yourself the MOST as explained in previous chapters.

11. Raise your inner demon from the hidden darkness through the process of alchemical activation, and allow it to sit side by side as the yin/yang, the sun and moon, so that your dark God/Goddess and light God/Goddess may be fully integrated into divine union.

12. YOU CANNOT do this on your own unless you have been chosen by the ancient ones. In this case, they will come in to teach you when you are ready. Get with someone who has already traveled this path to help you, such as Timmésha whom we have called, ordained, and allowed to write this book for you.

13. Know that by reading this book, you are already well on your way to doing the work to access, raise for activation, and unleash your suppressed superpower. If you were not, you would not have chosen to read this book.

14. This power is only made **super** by doing the inner work to raise it up to be crowned through your crown chakra. Otherwise, it is simply sitting, raw power that is waiting for you to refine it through the process of alchemical activation.

15. "Those whom God hath joined together let no man put asunder" (Matthew 19:6).

—The Ancient Ones, The Ancient Ancestors

Activate

DAWN.

This is the phase of your *rebirth*; think of it as your unveiling ceremony! Now that you have survived your dusk (i.e., the journey through your inner dark hell), you are prepared and well equipped to rise into the dawn of your new days, fully activated in all of your born-with-it power. Now that you have journeyed into your inner hell to retrieve your hidden in-the-dark and suppressed feminine God/Goddess (aka Demon, Savage, Devil, Moon), it is now time to raise her up into divine union to rule *alongside* her light counterpart (aka Masculine/God, Angel, and Sun) in holy matrimony. Think of the dusk journey as your process of mining for your own DNA-coded gold. Now consider your dawn phase as the process of bringing that gold to the surface. Also, for this next portion, I'd like you to keep in mind **the law of conservation of energy**: "*Energy can neither be created nor destroyed- only converted from one form to another.*"

Remember my sketch of the **suppressed seed-power** in chapter three? In this dawn phase, you will be guided to raise the power of that seed upward and outward; this is the dawning of your Phoenix, your fire, your power of the dark joined with light. I was guided to do some digging on the process of seed growth as it relates to actual farming and gardening. In my search, I found some details that I believe will help to parallel your journey through and out of the darkness (like the seed of a child planted in a mother's dark womb) to that of reaping and harvesting in the earth—with careful consideration to *your body being the earth of your inner world.*

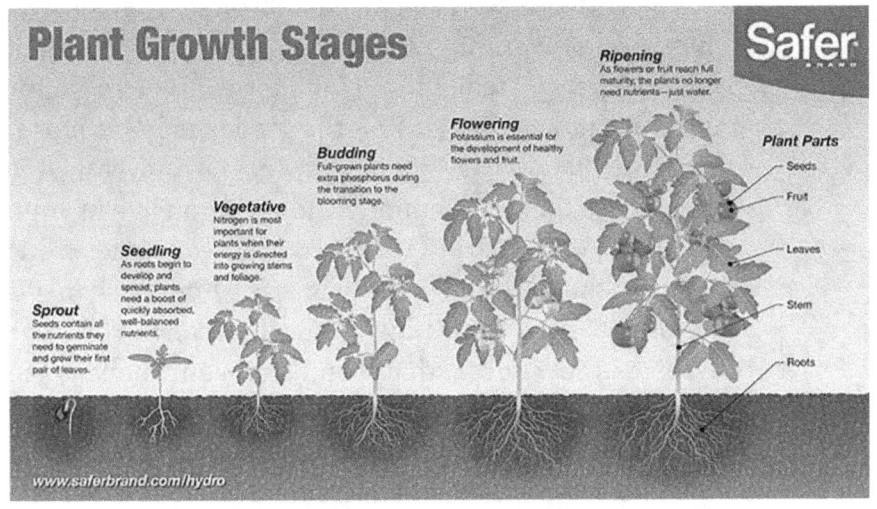

Image from www.saferbrand.com/articles/plant-growth-stages

Now out of all the online articles that described seed growth, I had to go with a write-up developed by a company called **Safer Brand**. To me, they outlined the phases of growth in a way I feel best aligns with the process of activation, and here's why. According to Safer Brand, there are six plant growth stages. Of course, I got excited when I read this because I'm automatically connecting the concept of our inner chakra systems. Now while there are seven primary chakras (*there are well over 100 chakra centers in and around the body*), the six stages still align when you consider the *seed* itself as the first stage, therefore making a total of seven stages; So let's begin.

Seven (7) stages on how to divinely activate, unleash, and raise hell. These stages will help guide you through practical methods to raise up your suppressed seed-power out of the darkness of hell from where it has been planted and into the light of your inner heaven for crowning.

Activate

1. **Seed (Root Chakra).** Keep in mind that your seed-power is always lying dormant within you, until you've done the inner work to raise it up to and through your crown chakra for activation. Yes, sexual trauma, and other forms of energy stealing and/or harvesting can smite your seed's power, but NEVER the seed itself. Therefore, do not fear that you are not able to regain your power, it is impossible that you cannot. As long as you live in your body, the seed *itself* from which your power comes from remains in the dark soil waiting to rise. Others may have attempted to steal your power, but they can never steal the seed—the source that conducts your power. At times, you may have felt powerless, but this was because your power energy may have been taken and/or given away. Once you *inner*stand and connect to the presence of your infinite seed, which is always producing power within you, the very idea of powerlessness will be a laughable folklore.

During root activation you will experience but not limited to the following:

- Impulses to want to have sex, because "down there" is where the feminine energy exists and has been trapped for centuries.

- Anger and frustration. Not because of blockage, but due to activating raw power that has been wrongfully accused and held hostage.

- Primal/raw desire

- Arousal.

- Do your research. Dig deep on what it may look like within your body when this root chakra is out of balance. Web searches delve deep into what it looks like when these areas are, as they say, "blocked." However, in this particular body of work, they are not just blocked but "out of order," out of service, misused, abused, and inactivated.

The issue over time has been that when we feel the onset of our power in our underworld, our vaginas, our PUSSIES or better known as our **root chakra**; we have been taught to pour it out onto a partner or shun it away altogether.

The journey through your shadow or inner dark work allows these primal emotions to rise. Allowing them to rise does not mean to unleash them just yet, quite the contrary! This power is much too primal to unleash without having first completed activation. When unleashed prematurely, we see toxic behaviors such as but not limited to attacking others due to jealousy, competing, and hating, or worse, such as those that attempt to use sex as a weapon for gain and control. To allow these emotions to rise means that the energy MUST be raised all the way up to and out of your crown *to be crowned*, so that you may be fully activated for mental health and refined for emotional intelligence. Through this work, you will learn the true meaning of the **G-spot**! Through full activation of all seven stages and beyond, you will innerstand that G-spot stands for "God spot" (i.e., the higher mind and/or inner heaven). When your true G-spot (higher mind or heaven where your inner god dwells) is tapped through the rise of your fires for activation to your crown, then and only then will you intrinsically feel, innerstand, *over*stand, the intensity of *"Mmmmm, that's the spot!"*

Practice method: Light a red candle, and meditate as often as you can over time, and envision your red seed pulsating with vibrant life.

It's important to note the symptoms you feel as they come up. However, for this particular body of work, note that as you start to awaken this energy you are going to feel impulses that feel like sexual urges, which we know only feels sexual because this is the center in which your power is. It has been suppressed within the body that this energy has just been sitting . . . until now.

When you feel that your body is wanting to move, allow it. This may look like spreading your legs, rotating your hips/pelvis clockwise and counterclockwise. This may also include bouncing your pelvis against the floor (straddle position). You may be guided to bounce hard enough (firmly) so that you can feel the vibration radiate through your pelvic floor. You will feel the arousal of her power as she rises up. When your body is ready, it will guide you on what to do to break up and shake free your trapped Goddess as she begins to rise. You will be guided on what movements to make to help set it/her/you free.

2. Sprout (Sacral Chakra). "Each seed contains a small parcel of nutrients that is all they need to germinate and begin growing their first pair of leaves" (Saferbrand.com).

As mentioned in number one's **seed stage**, you are now well aware of the fact that your seed contains the nutrients it needs to germinate. Germinate is defined as, beginning to grow and put out shoots after a period of dormancy. The synonyms include sprout, shoot up, bud, form/develop buds, develop, grow, spring up, swell.

Are you getting excited, or shall I say ***aroused***, yet by simply reading this portion? You should be! Your arousal is proof that your seed's power is brewing. The issue over time has been that when we felt or feel the onset of our power in our underworld, our wombs, our vaginas, our PUSSIES, better known as our **root and sacral chakras**, we either fucked it away—yes (sexed it away)—or kept it down, suppressed. Keeping it down is synonymous with pressing it back in or down, hence, the onset of depression. Instead, learn the different methods to cultivate your seed power as opposed to fucking it away or pushing it back down.

During sacral activation you will experience but not limited to the following:

- Impulses to want to have sex, because "down there" is where the feminine energy exists and has been placed for centuries.

- Creative sparks to develop and begin new projects. (You may suddenly decide to start drawing, writing, painting, singing, etc.)

- Emotional release (crying without an obvious reason). If you are an empath, you will feel deep emotions that are not always about you, but are happening through you. You will cry or purge energy that you are connecting to from the world around you. You will purge emotions that you may have held onto not just from this life, but from your past lives as well.

- Increased intuition and sensitivity. You will *feel* into what is and is not working for you more than *thinking* about it. However, continue to raise the power upward for emotional intelligence to ensure your feelings are intuitive and not based on fear.

- Do your research. Dig deep on what it may look like within your body when this sacral chakra is out of balance. Web searches will delve deep into what it looks like when these areas are "blocked." However, in this particular body of work to activate, it is not just blocked, it is "out of order," out of service, misused, abused, and inactivated.

Practice method: Light both your red and orange candles, and meditate as often as you can over time, and envision your seed beginning to sprout its roots within the dark soil of you. Try imaging the color of your seed as red when doing this practice; pay attention to how you feel and what visions and thoughts arise as you work through this practice. Keep a journal of your progress and of what comes up. Keep in mind that you may not have any visions or epiphanies at the time of your practice. However, insights may follow in the days to come and/or you may have dreams that provide you feedback about your process.

It's important to note the symptoms you feel as they come up, do the research on what it may look like within your body when this root chakra is out of balance. However, for this particular body of work, note that as you start to awaken this energy, ***arousal—the throbbing of your vagina or the rising of your penis—***will and MUST occur. DO NOT, I repeat DO NOT confuse this energy with thinking you are supposed to get rid or satisfy your arousal with the act of sex. Although sex is great between two consenting adults, we are getting to know and activating a power far beyond the sexual reach. Do not get rid of your inner goddess awakening as soon as you feel her waking up within you down there. Remember, you only feel her down there because that is where you have been taught to suppress her, and also down there (like in all soil), is where seeds must first take root. You will only smite yourself of your own power by pouring her out onto another. Thus, again, this will suppress and put your inner Goddess back to sleep, to lay dormant in the dark. She's been thrown away enough hasn't she? She is heartbroken by the way in which we've treated her thus far, do you agree?

3. Seedling (Solar Plexus Chakra). "As plants' roots develop and spread, a boost of quickly absorbed, well-balanced nutrients

fuels the rapid growth from spindly seedling to healthy plant"(Saferbrand.com).

Just as the seedling within you, during this stage of raising your seed-power, you will need a sufficient amount of nutrients to boost the growth of your power upward. What type of nutrients? The nutrients you have harnessed from your so-named sexual/sensual energy by not pouring it out via sex. I say "so-named" because this power really IS NOT sexual energy, but more the suppression of power in the lower body. Therefore, the confusion that this is sexual energy is only called sexual energy because below or "down there" is where humans have been taught to keep this power . . . until now. This is why I mentioned the article I wrote titled, "**The Power of Celibacy and Abstinence They Never Wanted You to Know**" in chapter two. This reservoir of stored so-called sexual energy is the *boost* you need to *arouse/swell* or give you a leg up, toward raising your power up to your next chakra for activation.

During solar plexus activation you will experience but not limited to the following:

- Impulses to enforce your power. But remember, the energy is still too raw to do so. This will only result in outward expressions of forcing your will on others.

- You will develop a strong sense of your born-with-it individual purpose and life's mission/calling. You will decide to deepen your studies on topics of interest.

- **Increase of what feels like anxiety.** This is because your risen dark Goddess fire is rising through your root, sacral, and now your solar for activation. This is almost like the colliding of multiple stars forming a supernova of power!

Activate

When you are activating at this phase, you may experience what feels like panic attacks. Why? Because at this point you have combined the activation powers of your root, sacral, now coming through to the solar plexus. The side effect of these activations feels like anxiety and/or panic attacks because it's really your divine Goddess raising her fire (i.e., raising hell) within you. You will feel a lot of heat, which feels like anxiety. This is what the world and clinical therapy approaches would call the symptoms of anxiety. However, what the world is calling anxiety is really this power wanting to come through and/or already coming through. It is the symptoms of power either wanting to activate or activating (if you are doing the inner work). You're going to feel that your body is getting overheated, even in moments of socially connecting. This why you will choose to isolate. You're going to feel that you're getting overheated, which is absolutely a GOOD SIGN and normal when you're on this journey to activate your mental health and emotional intelligence. This is a wonderful sign that your body is heated. It is letting you know that you have an immense amount of power that wants to be fully activated and/or is a sign that you are doing the work to move through your activation process. As you can see, it is important that you protect this process and protect others as this power is rising . . . because it is so powerful! What you don't want to do is burn others, right? What you don't want to do is set other people on fire—not yet, anyway. What I mean by not yet is that this heat and fire that you are feeling in your body is burning away everything that has been false, all of the masks. An example of this would be the burning of false friendships, relationships, jobs, false masks you've worn that are not you, and anyone that was never for you, and anything that never really was you. This burning is necessary for the stripping away of all things that have kept your power stuck, stagnant, hidden and suppressed. So, when you feel this fire rising, allow it to rise because it's doing its work within you—protect her and do not shun her because she burns. It's absolutely required. The Activate philosophy says, **LET IT BURN!** *Read from the practice method on what you can do to support yourself through this point.*

- Decide to isolate yourself from certain people, and places during this phase. This is wise only because of the fact that you are still learning to *be* and be with this newly awakened power. You must protect your growth at all costs from outside influences that may attempt to steal your newly risen power in its infancy. You must also isolate temporarily (how long will be up to your own growth process), because those around you WILL NOT understand your journey. Isolation is a good idea when you know you are on this particular journey to activate. You are protecting what's happening through and in you. You are protecting your seed power, which is much like protecting an infant. When a baby is in the womb, it is protected unless you do something to harm it yourself or if you allow someone to violate your womb, right? So, temporary self-isolation is required when on this journey of activating your suppressed superpower.

- Do your research. Dig deep on what it may look like within your body when this solar plexus chakra is out of balance. Web searches delve deep into what it looks like when this center is "blocked." However, in this particular body of work to activate, it is not just blocked, it actually has been "out of order," misused, abused, and out of service, and inactivated until now.

Practice method: Light a yellow candle and meditate as often as you can over time, and envision your seed power expanding as it receives the nutrients you stored up for it. Try imaging the color yellow pulsating and expanding when doing this practice. Pay attention to how you feel and what visions and thoughts come up as you work through this practice. Keep a journal of your progress and of what comes up. Keep in mind that you may not have any visions or epiphanies at the time of your practice; however, insights may follow in the days to come and/or you may have dreams that provide you feedback about your process.

For the rising of what feels like anger: SCREAM/YELL to efficiently stay with this power as it's doing its work in and through you. Scream, yell so loud that your veins begin to pop out of your neck and face. Scream to the point you feel satisfied. I can recall times I've screamed until I felt faint.

It's important to note the symptoms you feel as they come up, do the research on what it may look like within your body when this solar chakra is out of balance or is lacking energy. Remember the purpose of this practice is to raise your seed power up so that your solar chakra is no longer lacking energy.

4. **Vegetative (Heart Chakra).** "Nitrogen is a key component of chlorophyll, the green pigment in plants, so it's the critical

nutrient when their energy is focused on growing stalks and foliage" (Saferbrand.com).

Keep going! This is where you are going to see and feel your world not only shift within you, but you're going to see your world shift around you. How? You are going to start making critical moves and changes to the people, places, and things you used to know. Why? Because as your power begins to produce and multiply within this space, you will all of a sudden have a change of heart. This is where your emotional intelligence has been gained and will be further refined from this point upward. Not only are you now able to understand, but you will innerstand your emotions on a much deeper level. **See the relevance; vegetative = green = green heart chakra.**

When your heart changes, EVERYTHING changes within and without. This is where you will begin to see the saying, "As within, so without" come to life in your life!

At this stage you may find yourself feeling deeply into the power of the lyrics song so brilliantly by singer/songwriter *Adelle*;

"THERE'S A FIRE STARTING IN MY HEART, REACHING A FEVER PITCH AND IT'S BRINGING ME OUT THE DARK."

This fever or fire that Adelle speaks about is your once-suppressed superpower rising. Take Adelle for example as it relates to turning pain into power. She exemplifies what it looks like on the surface to set yourself ablaze with the power that we've all been taught to keep down under, hidden deep in our underworld.

During heart chakra activation you will experience but not limited to the following:

- A desire to laugh even when no one has said anything funny! YOU WILL LAUGH all by your damn self when you are in private and when you are in public, and no one would have said a damn thing funny to you. Why? Because the laughter will be the irony of all the fuckery that you are now seeing and feeling. The laughter will be indicative of all the hidden truths that are now made clear to you and through you. You will realize all of the falseness around you and all of the falseness you carried inside yourself. You will laugh from your heart because it will be a jovial coming-into of your power. You will laugh because you are activating ancient downloads/uploads wisdoms within you of hidden truths that will suddenly become obvious to you. When you come into the hidden truths of how good of a game they played, and how good they were at playing with your mind all these lifetimes and centuries, you will laugh at the apparent fuckery. You will laugh because you have now activated a power that finds it all quite comical.

- You will have less need to react and a more deeply intelligent desire to respond only if you absolutely MUST! Your newly gained emotional intelligence will be evident based on your power to make decisions from your heart space. But do not mistake your risen power into your heart for complete vulnerability. Quite the contrary, you will begin to feel from your heart based on all of your previously activated chakras, who and what should stay and who you absolutely must LET GO to protect this power's growing stage. This doesn't mean you build a wall. NO, there are no walls when you develop emotional intelligence; there are instead healthy boundaries finally established. Your risen Goddess will establish these boundaries from this place without you having to do much at all. Allow her risen essence to work within you and your higher-mind; she knows what to do.

- Refine your empathic abilities, thus become better able to feel love in a way that is otherworldly. You may feel like you have loved and been loved by a person you've never met in this lifetime. This stage is usually when you are able to recall past life loves, and are able to connect energetically to the person you may be destined for, whether you ever get the chance to meet them in this life or not. However, allow your own individual heart activation to tell you its once-hidden secrets now revealed only to you.

- Do your research. Dig deep on what it may look like within your body when the heart chakra is out of balance. Web searches delve deep into what it looks like when this center is as they say "blocked." However, in this particular body of work to activate, it is not just blocked, it actually has been "out of order," misused, abused, out of service, and inactivated until now.

Practice method: Light a green candle and meditate as often as you can over time, and envision your seed power vibrating upward and outward. See sparks of the color green popping outward from your chest as it receives the nutritional fire of the risen Goddess that has been suppressed below. Try imaging the color green pulsating and expanding within your chest as she sets your heart on fire, burning away all the bullshit your heart has taken over lifetimes. When doing this practice, pay attention to how you feel and what visions and thoughts come up as you work through this practice. Keep a journal of your progress and of what comes up. Keep in mind that you may not have any visions or epiphanies at the time of your practice, however, insights may follow in the days to come, and/or you may have dreams that provide you feedback about your process.

It's important to note the symptoms or side-effects you feel. Do the research on what it may look like within your body when this heart chakra is out of balance or lacking energy. Remember the purpose of this practice is to raise your seed power up so that your heart chakra is no longer lacking energy. Feel into this practice. Place your hand over your chest, try rubbing your hands together vigorously to warm them before placing them over your chest.

5. Budding (Throat Chakra). "Phosphorus is in extra high demand at the start of a plant's reproductive cycle, the transition from growing leaves to forming buds" (Smartbrand.com).

This stage of your seed-power, aka the raising of your hidden and suppressed goddess, is beginning to show herself to the outside world. Not only will you feel her, but the world will start to see her, which is essentially the "new you" showing up in the world. Others may say to you, "***You've changed or something is different about you.***" They may even say something about you is different and won't be able to quite put their finger on it. This is proof that your power is budding, showing up and being seen and felt by others around you.

However, do not stop your inner dark work just because you feel and the world is starting to see the new you. Many make this mistake of thinking the work is done, so cut her short. Do not cut yourself short of your full power. Remember the work is to fully integrate your dark goddess into the daily habits of your day. This work is an infinite process of integrating both your underworld and your outer world.

During throat chakra activation you will experience but not limited to the following:

- STRONG impulses to call people and things out on all of their bullshit before thinking and feeling your thoughts through to completion. But remember, this energy is still too raw to do so. This will only result in outward expressions of thoughts communicated from unrefined anger. Instead, continue to be guided to rising higher. Trust that you will always be internally guided on the most efficient and surest ways to cut poison out of your life, in a way that they can NEVER return or be redeemed.

- Begin to speak in a new way. You will speak the ancient language of your inner dark Goddess. You will know when you are speaking this language because others will look at you strangely or respectfully. They will either innerstand or withdraw from the ancient source from which you speak. Either way, allow your new language to develop over time because your newly rising power will speak in ways your former self is not used to. It will feel like a lost language; and I don't mean you'll automatically start speaking German if your mother tongue is Spanish. I mean that this ancient language comprises words of profundity spoken from a place of deeply rooted wisdom and insight that hasn't been spoken within you for centuries. Either way, be guided to look up words that come to you if you are not clear of their definition or if you require deeper insight into what this language is wanting to communicate through you. An example of this will be that at times you may be simply washing dishes, and all

Activate

of a sudden a word will drop into your deeper mind out of the blue. Go immediately if you can and look up the definition of this word, even if you think you already know the definition, look it up. There is always something deeper for you to know that your newly awakened dark Goddess is urging to speak through you. Look at all the synonyms and every component of the defined description of the word.

- Begin writing and speaking or evolve in your communication style. You may even desire to learn a foreign language.

- Find yourself speaking to yourself, yes! Talking to yourself. This is truly a conversation happening between you and your most infinite self. Enjoy these times, and allow your communication to evolve as it wishes. You will find yourself communicating more deeply with your spirit guides, ancestors, and so forth. Keep in mind that your spirit guides will evolve in their forms of communications with you.

- Be guided to say things that in the past you would have normally trained yourself not to say; you will be guided to speak truths you've once hidden.

- Do your research. Dig deep on what it may look like within your body when this throat chakra is out of balance. Web searches delve deep into what it looks like when this center is as they say "blocked." However, in this particular body of work to activate, it is not just blocked, it actually has been "out of order," misused, abused, and out of service, and inactivated until now.

Practice method: Light a light blue candle and meditate as often as you can over time, and envision your seed power rising and expanding your throat center. Try imaging the color light blue pulsating and expanding when doing this practice. Pay attention to how your throat area feels and what visions and thoughts come up as you work through this practice. Keep a journal of your progress and of what comes up. Keep in mind that you may not have any visions or epiphanies at the time of your practice. However, insights may follow in the days to come and/or you may have dreams that provide you feedback about your process.

It's important to note the symptoms you feel as they come up, do the research on what it may look like within your body when this throat chakra is out of balance or is lacking energy. Also look up what it looks like when this energy center is "IN BALANCE," as it is now receiving and being empowered by the once lowered Goddess energy from your underworld.

6. Flowering (Third Eye Chakra). "Potassium plays a primary role in producing and transporting the sugars and starches plants use up as they develop healthy flowers and fruit" (Amartbrand.com).

Your rising power is now fully seen and flowering, meaning, there is no doubt that you are producing something those around you have never seen before. Your once suppressed power has now risen into your inner mind.

During third eye chakra (pineal gland) activation you will experience but not limited to the following:

- Deeper intuitive insights, dreams, and visions. Be sure to journal them as often as you receive and remember them. It's best not to wait to do this, because oftentimes the potency of the message may begin to subside from your conscious mind. Remember, it is your hidden self that is attempting to communicate with you from the dark, so don't forget to write down her messages. When she rings, don't miss the call . . . answer!

- You will notice increased synchronicity such as repeating numbers, colors, animals, songs, music, etc.

- Recalling your past lives, and recalling your past lives' gifts.

- Will be able to see with your inner eye if people are trustworthy, authentic, and transparent.

- You will see, feel, and know many things beyond the superficial and beneath the surface.

- Increased intuition, insight, clairvoyance, and empathic knowing—so much so that you may decide to further isolate yourself from others and from places because you are able to read and see into people and places where deception is CLEAR. Not assumed, but clear evidence will be present through intuitive sparks and empathic nudges that make you deeply uncomfortable around certain people and places.

- You may even decide to honor your third eye by placing a bhindi or other form of colored paint. (Note: You will not do this for style, but for the sake of honoring that which is often unseen and under-represented.)

- Do your research. Dig deep on what it may look like within your body when this third eye chakra is out of balance. Web searches delve deep into what it looks like when these areas are as they say "blocked." However, in this particular body of work to activate, it is not just blocked; it is "out of order," misused, abused, out of service, and inactivated.

Practice method: Light a dark blue candle and meditate as often as you can over time, and envision your seed power vibrating within your forehead. See sparks of indigo/dark blue popping outward from your forehead as it receives the activation power from your Goddess risen from your underworld. Try imaging the color indigo blue pulsating and expanding around your forehead as you feed your mind with the energy you've risen up into it. When doing this practice, pay attention to how you feel and what ideas and thoughts come up as you work through this practice. Keep a journal of your progress, and write out all that comes up over time. Keep in mind that you may not have any visions or epiphanies at the time of your practice. However, insights may follow in the days to come and/or you may have dreams that provide you feedback about your process.

It's important to note the symptoms or side effects (insights) you feel or are seeing as they come up. Do the research on what it may look like within your body when this third-eye chakra is out of balance or is lacking energy. Remember the purpose of this practice is to raise your seed power up so that your third eye chakra is no longer lacking energy.

7. Ripening (Crown Chakra). "When flowers and fruit are verging on full maturity, they need a week or two of just water without nutrients, a process known as "flushing," so they can use up all of the nutrients they have already absorbed" (Smartbrand.com).

Activate

During crown chakra activation you will experience but not limited to the following:

- A crowing-like sensation surrounding the top of your head. It may feel like someone has placed an invisible crown around the top portion of your head (at least this was the experience in my case). You may feel the top of your scalp tingle. Allow this and pay attention to what visions or insights come up over time.

- Be internally guided on what and how to speak, write, and eat, where to go, what to do, and with whom to connect to.

- Alignments with people, places, and things that match your newly risen power. They will mirror back to you the same risen power because they will see and feel you and you them.

- Seemingly connect and commune with animals, and they will commune with you. In fact, all of nature will communicate with you and you with it.

- Be inclined to study the cosmos and other life forms not of planet earth.

- Have a strong desire to travel. This is because your newly risen power knows there is more beyond your day-to-day that you will need for wellness. It knows where it needs to go to receive the desired resources it needs to thrive. An example would be to have the desire to travel to Costa Rica. Although you've never been, your newly risen self may know that Costa Rica contains minerals in its soil that you need to thrive, heal, and/or recharge your now awakened superpower.

- Do your research. Dig deep on what it may look like within your body when this crown chakra is out of balance. Web searches will delve deep into what it looks like when these areas are as they say "blocked." However, in this particular body of work to activate, it is not just blocked, it is "out of order," misused, abused, out of service, and inactivated.

Practice Method: Just allow, journal what comes up, and follow suit what you are guided to do, undo, become, and unbecome.

Keep in mind that as your dark Goddess/suppressed feminine power has risen to your crown to be crowned, she has activated each chakra center on her ascension. If you do this inner work over time, you will have gained your mental health and will have refined your emotional intelligence through each stage of the fire activation of the risen dark Goddess. Each point of activation mirrors back to you as the experiencer, impulses that look a lot like the symptoms of what the world has labeled as depression, anxiety, and suicidal ideation. If you truncate the rise of your seed power by neglecting this inner work, then mental health and emotional intelligence will not be gained. Remember that this activation of your seed power is what is making your power "***super***," hence superpower. Moreover, when your risen Goddess has reached your crown chakra to be crowned, she is now integrated with none other than her divine counterpart, better known as God. This is the point where Father God and Mama Goddess are once again joined together in divine union—it is the marriage between both your dark and light, yin and yang, angel and demon, sun and moon, God and Devil.

Activate

The most crucial point to make at this final (yet not so final) phase of the seven (7) stages is **protection**. Because I was guided to incorporate the farming and gardening process of seed growth, let me lastly include the ABSOLUTE, non-compromising, unquestionable need to safeguard your shit! Here's what I mean.

According to **Safer Brand** on the stages of plant growth,

> During the stages of plant growth, you can focus on getting the best results at the end of the season by utilizing an arsenal of tools to defend your plants against pests and diseases . . . Between the stages of vegetation and ripening, your plants might be attractive to different pests . . . It's important to pay attention to the ripening stage of your plants, as you don't want ready-to-harvest vegetables to get sabotaged in the last growth stage! (Saferbrand.com).

Oh wee, when I read the above information on Saferbrand.com, I yet again felt aroused! Remember, that arousal is simply your body responding to the enlightenment of profound truth activated within you. Once you know this, what are you going to do with this ancient wisdom? Well, I'll tell you what I did on my journey through the darkness of my mental and emotional health. I armored up! I allowed my darkness now integrated with my light to guide me on the best and most efficient way to protect my now activated power and the fruits of my laborious growth.

DO NOT mistake the fact that as you start to produce healthy fruits such as but not limited to creative ideas that inspire the masses, innovative solutions that solve world problems, and building spaceships so you can visit your ancient ancestors on Venus, that just like normal plants, trees, and crops that begin to flourish, you WILL ATTRACT pests, locusts, and weeds of all kinds. Weeds whose job it is to choke out your seed and usurp your harvests for all the life they have in them. These pests show up in what looks like **naysayers, haters**; those that will attempt to **sabotage your efforts** or **belittle your mission**, those that will attempt to **kill, destroy**, and **steal from you**; those that will indeed seek to **tarnish your image, slander your name**; those that will *attempt to* **befriend you for selfish gain**; and even those that will **attempt to get romantically involved** in hopes of basking in all you've worked for. But do not fret, realize that this too is a normal progression of life as we have already seen with the farming outline. No matter what, your now integrated dark and light will in no way allow you to be killed, stolen from, or destroyed again! Be sure to call on your ancestors, spirit guides, and whatever or whoever you trust in the unseen realms for added protection. You will need them! Remember that on this path of reawakening your sleeping deity within and activating your superpower for mental and emotional health; attacks against you are what call you to awaken to who and what you are, and your power. This is proof that what you have inside you, is delectable and attractive to opposing forces. Note that serious attacks against you and your DNA-coded gifts is what qualifies you as a chosen one. No matter what, I and the world cannot wait to see what you've been hiding underneath your pain and trauma all this time.

Can you think of times in your life when someone, a group of people, or something attempted or succeeded in hindering your growth? If so, what did you learn and *unlearn* from those experiences?

CHAPTER 5: MENTAL DISORDERS & THE CHOSEN ONES

If you are one of the chosen ones, you must go through intense, life-shifting, mind-altering pains! Why? Because you'll have nothing to offer the world in the realm of extraordinary without having done so. There's just NO WAY around it! These pains and going through hell is what equips you for your destiny as a chosen one. You're probably wondering, **how can all the pain you've been through make you a chosen one?**

The answer is simple, yet not so simple; because you were tried by the fire!

The journey is to **(re)member** from "**dismemberment**." You were dismembered (*cut off the limbs of, pull apart, cut up, chop up, break up, dissect, divide, segment, mutilate, hack up, butcher, tear limb from limb*), torn apart, and scattered from your power, thus dismembering the truth of who and what you are. Your work as a chosen one is to (re)member (put back together) your mind, emotions, and power from dismemberment; It is the (re)membering of all that you are. Anxiety, depression, and suicidal thoughts are the symptoms or side-effects that the chosen ones MUST experience as a kind of fail-safe (*pertaining to or noting a mechanism built into a system, as in an early warning system . . . for ensuring safety should the system fail to operate properly*), that signals the body when its trapped power is attempting to reorganize all scattered parts of itself.

On this journey of activation and knowing who and what you are, you begin to thank... literally be thankful that the symptoms of anxiety, depression, and suicidal thoughts showed up at all for you. Why? Because you realize that if they hadn't, you would have never been awakened to your power, purpose, and reason for being born at all. I know some of us would say, **"Well why did I have to go through all of this, couldn't I have just known and bypassed all of this shit?"** My response to this question would be the same response that came to me, **"There is no such thing as light without dark."** Yes, I was irritated as FUCK when I got this response from within, but I knew that based on this earthly, dense, 3D realm in which we all are living and having this human experience, there is just no such thing as gain without pain. Could some pains have been avoided? Sure! But, remember that when you are born into this world, there are just some things that are out of your control. Thankfully this idea of turning pain into power is REAL, and through this written work you and those that come after you will forever have the tools to alchemize shit into sunshine.

Activate

The above wisdom came to me some time in the early part of 2020, after one of my many meditations and chats I was having with my ancestors and the ancient ones one night. I was crying on the floor—not because I was sad, but because I was angry, frustrated, and annoyed by all that I realized has been hidden from the world. Perhaps some of what was hidden was for good reason as it relates to those with mental illness accessing ancient wisdom only to overpower others. However, if this was the reason, I'd say the mission was incomplete and failed miserably! Because those that hid the knowledge of self in scrolls and secret societies were some of the ones whose aim it was to usurp power. Nevertheless, let's continue.

The truth of the matter is that those that hid the knowledge of individual power in scrolls didn't know that there was also knowledge hidden from them! The gag is (in my Keke Palmer voice), that we, "the chosen ones," were also hidden for a time or times such as these. A time when chaos, destruction, and subterfuge would be unleashed on the planet in such a way, that only those born DNA-coded with wisdom would have the insight, intuition, and spiritual gifts to build anew. What they also didn't know was that the key to unlocking us was pain, betrayal, and chaos—how clever the ancient ones were and are! To further drive home this point, I will allow the ancient wisdom to be activated within me to speak as usual, I can only share it the way it's activated within me.

Activated/Downloaded/Uploaded/Channeled Message

We knew that their thirst for blood would overtake them and that you would always be their prey. You were their prey because you were naturally born with what they wished they could possess. And so, because they did not naturally possess it they sought to possess you who were born with it. We could not leave you empty handed although it appeared we did. Your evolution was your own and we could not interfere; however, we systemized a fail-safe within many of you 144. Because we knew they would inflict pains upon you, we built within your DNA a switch that would reawaken you to your powers. So when they did transgress upon you, your switch would be activated; thus turning on your UNFUCKWITHABLE superpower. They are not aware that the more pain they inflict, the more formidable you become. Yes, it had to be this way for there could have been no other way that you could defend yourselves until our return. Not only are you able to defend yourselves, but you will be able to storm kingdoms *without* force. Your activations will be enough to send them running for the hills; thus, being able to reclaim your thrones as rulers and leaders of yourselves.

—The Ancient Ones

As a chosen one you may have

1. Survived sexual traumas
2. Endured vicious and unjustified slander, mockery, hate, death threats, and betrayal
3. Opted for singlehood (unmarried)
4. Hit "rock bottom" (more than once)

5. Been called to fulfill, create, and birth unique (*special, eccentric, isolated, single, unrepeatable, exclusive, one and only, in a class by itself, rare, uncommon, unusual, peculiar, strange, odd*) missions
6. Contemplated suicide or had thoughts of death

Surviving sexual traumas

Now don't get me wrong, I'm in no way suggesting that being raped or molested makes you a chosen one, absolutely not! For this particular body of work, I am saying that sexual trauma is only substantial *proof* that what dwells within you is worth so much that many over time have sought to **control it, buy it, sell it, steal it** from you through sexual exploitation or have even attempted to **kill you for it**. Make sense? There's no need to re-explore the acts of sexual trauma. You can scroll back to chapter two for that insight if you feel the need. However, I am being guided to express to you that you not only survived it, but you now know for sure that what you carry within you is not pain from the trauma, but pain indicative of a power kept hidden and masked underneath all the trauma. After you take the journey through your inner dark to activate your suppressed superpowers, I cannot wait to see what you've been hiding all this time!

Endured vicious and unjustified slander, mockery, hate, death threats and betrayal

As chosen ones we live on the planet with 7.5 billion other people, and because we are empaths, clairvoyant, clairaudient, psychic, intuitive and can feel and sense things on deep levels, it's important to know that it will be difficult to not see the faces or hear the judgments, the mocking and scoffing of others that we all must live among. So because of this, and because you now know that you are a chosen one due to your DNA-coded gifts, you must choose to be **comfortable** with how **uncomfortable** you

are going to feel that others are *uncomfortable* with you (*read that part several times so that it sinks in*). Because you can feel into the energies of those that are truly for you and/or against you, choose right now that you are going to allow your emotional intelligence to train you on how to be comfortable with how uncomfortable you are going to feel that others will hate and hate on you.

When I came into the knowledge of who and what I am as a spiritually gifted one, I realized why I was afraid to come into the light with all of my superpower exposed. I uncovered through my dusk journey that I feared not only being ridiculed for my gifts, but that I could be killed for them as well. During my dusk phase, I recalled my past lives where I was killed by the same people who loved me for my spiritual wisdom but also hated me for the same. I innerstood why that episode of *Penny Dreadful* of the witches hanging and burning spoke to me in such a way; I literally fell to my living room floor bent over and sobbing in tears. It was as if I was looking at a life I and so many had once lived before—like I was reliving a pain I knew all so well. I faced a grueling hard truth while journeying through why anxiety, depression, and suicidal thoughts showed up for me—it was because I wanted to remain unseen due to mockery, unheard due to slander, and unfelt due to sexual trauma—this in-turn kept me broke, and broken mentally, emotionally, and financially.

As chosen ones we are equipped to handle what would be attacks from others because we've endured them all before in this lifetime and past ones. I know that there will be some who will not like what I've outlined in this book, and that there will be some brave but stupid ones who will even attempt to discredit it. I've been well briefed by my spirit guides that there will always be death threats on the lives of the chosen, but those attacks will fail. Why? Because we've been there and done that already. We've been hung, stoned, raped, mocked, ridiculed, and burned, and those days are done! Remember in earlier chapters where I mentioned that this intelligent power has evolved and will never allow herself to be misused or abused again? In this fact, we can rest assured that there will be no power outside of ourselves that could ever succeed in scattering us or our purposes again. The ancient ones aren't having it either way.

The lessons I have learned from uncovering my "hidden in the dark" truths as a chosen one were as follows:

1. Keep my circle small, and even then be mindful of the small circle.

2. Make sure those that I support don't have direct access to me.

3. Only congregate among like-spirited ones who I *intuitively know* I don't have to watch my back around.

Now these are my truths, I am in no way suggesting that you follow suit on the same principles. But for my particular journey, it has been crucially important that I maintain certain boundaries as it relates to my wellbeing, safety, and the safety of my family and loved ones.

With my truths in mind, what boundaries have you been called to set to ensure your mental health and emotional intelligence? List three below, or if you are reading this in eBook version, then write them in your journal or on a separate sheet a paper. Channel *Gabrielle Union* **in tv series "***Being Mary Jane***", and place sticky notes around your home if you have to, to remind yourself daily of the new decisions your activated self now makes.**

Boundary #1. _____

Boundary #2. _____

Boundary #3. _____

Timmesha Burgess

Opted for singlehood (unmarried)

As a chosen one you will choose to remain single or unmarried unless you meet others that are on the same like-minded calling missions and purposes. Why? Because as a chosen one, you must first know what your individual mission is so that you will not be dismayed or disillusioned when you meet others. As a chosen one, you will know that your missions must align with those of the people with whom you are destined to cross paths. If you have not yet come into knowledge of yourself and individual power through alchemical activation, how can you possibly know the other to which you have attached yourself. Chosen ones know that they must first know themselves (meaning their purpose and power) before they can ever know another.

Singlehood is the surest way that the chosen ones come into knowledge and full alignment of their individual missions before ever joining forces with a romantic other. On my personal journey, I can attest that if I had been in a romantic partnership before my journey to activation, I would never have come into my power, at least not in this lifetime. I often say to my family that I AM NOT coming back to this planet and doing this shit again. If anyone wants to find me, they will have to find me on planet Venus getting fed grapes by some sexy god named Zeus. HA! Transparently speaking, many of us chosen ones failed to adhere to our individual purposes because many of us who opted for relationships in our past lives were always too immersed in going on dates, cooking, hanging out at their place and with friends for sporting events, so on and so forth. I never would have been alone long enough to even have remotely come close to listening deep within myself. I would not have had the gumption to attune deeply within myself to uncover that I was a reincarnation yet back on earth again because I didn't fulfil what I was meant to in my previous lifetimes. I would never have known my own individual prowess because I would have been too consumed in ensuring he was happy. As I and many have done for others throughout our entire lives. As aunts, sisters, mothers, daughters, sons, fathers, our entire lives are usually wrapped up in ensuring the satisfaction of everyone else but our own. However, this mission supersedes satisfaction on a mundane level, this journey is the path to satisfaction for the souls retrieval. As in the words of the late great **Bob Marley,** "Satisfy my soul."

Chosen ones may eventually decide to enter into a commitment with those that are of the same missions. However, this should only happen when they are guided into union by their ancestors. No family, friend, or colleague can convince them otherwise. Your spirit guides will send signs that they want you to join in union with someone, and this will be them working to soften you for romance. Why? Because when you know the truth of who you are and what you are born to do, you want no one and nothing to break your focus. This is how serious you as a chosen one will be about completing your born-with-it purpose and mission. You will know when your ancestors have guided someone into your life, because he or she will remind you of your power and of yourself. They will mirror back to you as proof that they too have journeyed the same path through the darkness, and will reflect your power. In the words of **Erykah Badu**, "*Many nights he was alone . . . his light was too bright so they turned away and he stood alone every night and every day. Then he turned to me, he saw his reflection in me. And he smiled at me, when he turned to me, then he said to me . . . how good it is.*"

Until then, please understand, innerstand, and *over*stand that singlehood is a powerful and necessary tool when you know that you are DNA-coded to fulfill divine missions. You KNOW without a doubt that you are an actual activated Goddess that can only join missions with an activated God—and that you are a God that can only join missions with a Goddess.

Hit "rock bottom" (more than once)

Most people hit rock bottom and immediately try to rebuild based on all the principles they used before. However, when we, the chosen ones, hit rock bottom for the umpteenth time in our lives, we finally are led to ask the question, "**Damn I'm down here again, wait what the heck is this rock actually**?" When the chosen ones ask this, we do more than just try to get out, we start to examine the actual rock for what it is. And all of a sudden have an epiphany to start chipping away at the rock, why? We are the ones guided to chip away at the rock in order to build the new from among the rubble of which we've broken through. The thing is, the you that fell down into rock bottom is not the same you that breaks up the rock to build anew. However, it's the new you that does this work. Because when you fell, the old you was destroyed and was broken at landing. This rock bottom was so hardcore, so harsh that it literally broke you. Many people like to sugarcoat falling by saying, "**Yeah, but it didn't break me.**" Well, on this journey through the dark . . . YOU MUST BREAK! You must be broken for the new you to emerge out through the brokenness and into the dawn of your new days. The old you would not be able to handle this new that you are being called to create, to build, to innovate; so I like to think of the old me as the *sacrificial lamb*. The old me that had to die so that my new, hidden, suppressed, and vilified me could be born.

This is where the chosen ones may begin to consider the idea of suicide or having suicidal thoughts. We'll talk more about suicidal ideations in the next point, but for now it's imperative to note that here, in the dusk phase, is where the chosen ones truly think about taking their own life. In this particular body of work, I delve deep into the new-age philosophy that suicidal thoughts for those activating their suppressed superpower is normal and necessary for the badass to be unleashed. Just for reference for those of you new to this concept, suicidal thoughts on this journey indicates that the new you is ready to have her/his day in the sun. These thoughts simply mean that you are ready to die to the old you, the false masks, beliefs, and traditions that once kept your true self hidden—no funeral arrangements needed! Not unless you want to hold a cool ritual-like ceremony to honor the death of the old you and the birth of the new you, kind of like when people hold divorce parties. If you do, make sure I get an invitation and I AM THERE, fully decked out in my bells and whistles!

Continue reading on to the chapter on suicide for further insight

Anyway, most hit rock bottom and focus on the fall, the pain, and the hitting of the hard surface. But the chosen ones hit and their focus is called to what is unleashed through the brokenness. There is something and someone that is released through the brokenness, and chosen ones who were once hidden ask, "**What and who is this emerging from the crack?**" The chosen ones know that the broken body and mind cannot build anew, NO! They innerstand that they have unleashed a power that supersedes the need to mend the old, when you can just build anew. It is a lot like when you crack open the genie bottle in the movies and then the genie is unleashed; well lo and behold, the genie in the goddamn bottle was you all along.

So, when this *hidden-in-the-bottle* (i.e., hidden-in-the-body) you is set free, it is this *you* that builds anew. This *you* will build your new world with all of the rocks that were thrown at you and also with the rocks that you gathered from chipping away at the rock in "rock bottom." So, for the chosen ones, this new is built on a completely solid foundation, and how do you know it's solid? Because it's fucking ROCK BOTTOM! If there's one thing you know for sure, it's that this new world you get to build is going to be as solid as a rock, because it's made out of it.

This new you can see in ways your old self could not or was not equipped to see before. This new you not only knows to chip away at the rock and then use the chipped debris to build, but this new you also discovers what was once hidden within the rock itself. Now we're talking, right? So let's journey even deeper into the dark.

As this newly unleashed you begins to chip away at the rock of "rock bottom," it notices something—shiny something(s) buried beneath the core. And what are those shiny something(s)? Your DNA-coded gold and your diamonds baby, yep! Your diamonds in the rough, your gold in the mine of your rock bottom. WOW! And according to the age-old sayings, "***Diamonds are forever and gold is precious.***" The chosen one's duty is to descend down into the rock bottom place over and over and over again, until we realize that what we've built from before was not our individual gold and diamond but rather all the false premises, beliefs, and traditions that we were taught to cling to since coming into the world. Our treasures lie hidden and buried among the rocks, so if you're down in your rock bottom at this point in your life, GET TO CHIPPING! Become the architect of your own life, and use those chipped pieces of rock to build your own way up and out, such as rising up like a seed from the earth fully in your own power.

Activate

Image from
https://www.reddit.com/r/bonehurtingjuice/comments/d0xd38/never_dont_give_up/

Now on the surface, others may see you differently, chosen ones! Yes, they will say, "*He/she has lost in life... They have lost it all and even their minds.*" I knew there were many that attempted to take a peek into my life from the outside trying to look in to make their assumptions about what they thought based on what they could and mostly could NOT see. There were many that mocked my struggle when my mother was wrongfully convicted and sent to prison, many that speculated based on the rumors that were spread about me when women gathered to blacklist me and sabotage my business reputation in my work space. There were also many that spread vicious rumors and gossip about my well-being and about my personal life that had never even met me, but gathered lies from those (the ones I got rid of) who wished they still had access to my life.

During the time I was hitting what looked like "rock bottom" for me, my middle sister Jessica was turning a new leaf in her life. When she decided to move to Atlanta from Miami and stay with me, I remember saying to her about a year later, "**Listen sis, I don't know what's going to happen because some things are changing in my life . . . I don't know what's going to happen, but I know that I won't be able to hold it all up like I have been much longer. You think you'll be able to handle it when this change happens, because I can feel it?**" Every time I asked her she would say, "**I got it, sis, everything will be okay.**" I remember feeling deeply that there was a change in the wind, and it was calling my name. I knew that wherever I was being called that I did not have the mental or emotional space to deal with the outside world too. Why? Because my world within needed my *undivided* (pun intended) attention. My sister moving to Atlanta was a part of a series of "*just right on time*" events for me, because as I was going into this place, there was no way that I could give anything to anyone else. I had nothing else to give. I had for so long given to people, places, and things that it had completely drained me of all I had, and they enjoyed doing it! It was as if everyone around me had gotten out of me everything they wanted to get, and then I became disposable. As a chosen one, you learn that what they thought was your value, and what they thought they were sponging from you and harboring for themselves, was merely the shadow of your power not yet fully emerged on the surface.

The ancient ones designed and hid the chosen ones so well among the others, that when those that sought to usurp you for all they thought you had showed up, they realized and you too realized that they were merely chasing the shadow of something much more profound not yet fully unleashed. OH, THE CLEVERNESS OF THOSE ANCIENTS! But know this, chosen ones, was all for your own protection, because had they known before who and what you really were, they would have kept up the masks of pretending to like you just so they could eat off the fruit of your harvests. So you see, you had to fall, hit rock bottom, be betrayed, slandered, and mocked, because only then would it be made clear to you who was truly for you when you appeared to have lost it all and who gathered kindling to help burn you at the stake.

So, chosen ones rising up out of rock bottom is solely because you were able to build from solid rock all that is true to you, immovable, unshakeable, un-stealable, and UNFUCKwithable. Because what you are coming out with is individual to you, and activated by you and you alone—no one will be able to activate that which you discovered from your rock bottom rubble because only you can do that. It came out of your rock not anyone else's. So, when others attempt to duplicate or steal what you create, it is to their own detriment. What you come out of the darkness with, came from your rock bottom. It is solid, having been gained and earned through your own alchemical death and rebirth.

Now listen to this, the diamond and gold buried within your rock bottom is ANCIENT. Why? Because that is where artifacts are discovered, buried deep beneath the rocky earth right? Your gold and diamonds are literally historical artifacts waiting for your discovery. Literally you will say, "***Oh, these are my treasures buried within this rock, damn this is some ancient shit! I'm bringing this back to the surface!***" And you'd be correct! This is the notion of ancient wisdom and intelligence being activated from within you, so that you may then share it with the world at the appointed time, having been guided and protected by your spirit guides to do so. The chosen ones are the ones called to fulfill and create **ancient practices**, **develop unique philosophies**, **build innovative solutions**, and to **create their own worlds** within worlds. May no thing, no one, no man, and no woman stand in your way!

Timmesha Burgess

Been called to fulfill, create, and birth unique missions

I remember reading a story once about a woman who was about to give birth to a son. The story goes as such:

> There was a woman who was clothed with the sun, and the moon was under her feet. She was pregnant and cried out with pain because she was about to give birth ... There was a giant red dragon there ... It stood in front of the woman who was ready to give birth to the baby. It wanted to eat the woman's baby as soon as it was born. The woman gave birth to a son, who would rule all the nations with an iron rod. And her child was taken up to God and to his throne. The woman ran away into the desert to a place that God had prepared for her. Then there was a war in heaven. Michael and his angels fought against the dragon. The dragon and its angels fought back, but they were not strong enough. The dragon and its angels lost their place in heaven. It was thrown down out of heaven to the earth. The dragon saw that he had been thrown down to the earth. So he chased the woman who had given birth to the child. But the woman was given the two wings of a great eagle. Then she could fly to the place that was prepared for her in the desert. There she would be taken care of for three and a half years. There she would be away from the dragon. Then the dragon poured water out of its mouth like a river. It poured the water toward the woman so that the flood would carry her away. But the earth helped the woman (Revelations, Chapter 12).

I read this story for the first time as an adult in 2021, when we talked about it on my mother's online broadcast called

Shifting Religious Concepts (SRC). At the time, we were studying the Book of Revelations not as religious folks, but because we were called to break down the allegory of biblical stories as it relates to shifting perspectives contrary to how we were taught in religious doctrine.

When we read this chapter of Revelations I remember feeling literally a bundle of joy tumble within me. I realized that I was the woman in the story, called to give birth not to a human child but to my DNA-coded missions, purpose, and this written body of work, and that like in the woman's story. I too had been hunted/haunted by the red dragons within other people. Remember, as was explained in the previous chapters, that the devil, beast, Savage in others are the only evil that seek to kill you, steal from you, and destroy you. Even when they attempt to use spell work (backward alchemy) to harm you by conjuring energies, they are still the ones that have positioned themselves to kill what you birth. Who are they, you wonder? Well, as I mentioned in the **seven (7) stages of seed-power growth for mental health and emotional intelligence**, "they" are the ones we know as haters, naysayers, former friends turned frenemy, and those that perpetuate competition, jealousy, and rivalry.

As the story mentions the color of the dragon, do you remember in the **seven (7) stages of seed-power growth for mental health and emotional intelligence,** where I mentioned the root chakra, can you recall the color of the root chakra? Yes, it is represented by the color red.

Based on what you learned about the root chakra in the seven (7) stages, what do you intuitively innerstand about the *red dragon* in the story of the woman?

- What does the color red represent?
- What does the dragon represent?

- How does the red dragon represent unrefined power not risen through the process of alchemical activation?
- What have you been called to give birth to that the dragons in others have attempted to kill in you?
- How do you relate to the woman in this allegorical story?

Visit Revelations, chapter 12, verse 1, and allow the following photo to provide you with a visual interpretation. **Write about the insights that come to you on the following two pages provided below.** *If you are reading this in eBook version, then use a separate sheet of paper.*

Activate

BIRTHING SUPERPOWER AND THE RED DRAGON PRACTICE

Image from https://www.behance.net/gallery/84671589/The-Woman-and-the-Dragon

Like the woman in the story, I too (as many of you have or will be) were ushered into the darkness on purpose—into the wilderness as a safe-haven. You realize that as a chosen one that the darkness, the journey into hell, was exactly the saving grace you needed to protect you and which you are to birth from the inactivated dragons in other people. The unrisen dragons in others know better than to even attempt to follow you into the wilderness, because in their attempt they would be gobbled up by whatever lived there. Meaning, because they were only operating from their lower selves, they would not have had the divine keys, only gained by integrating both higher and lower (light and dark) to survive. Because to withstand that path you have to be divinely called to activate or to even survive it; therefore, they know they are nowhere near equipped for the real wild. So, instead of taking the journey into their own darkness themselves and rising for activation with their power truly crowned, they seek to steal yours or destroy it.

We as women and men give birth to a lot more than just children. We give birth to our DNA-coded dreams, spiritually guided ideas, and divine missions. When you are in the process of carrying these ideas through conception, and right when you are about to give birth to your purpose in the world, there seems to be people, places, circumstances, and things that attempt to smite your seed from you. So, in order to ensure the safe delivery of your seed's power, IT IS REQUIRED THAT YOU JOURNEY INTO THE DARK WILDERNESS (i.e., your inner hell). All of our lives we have been taught to avoid going to hell, haven't we? However, for the chosen ones, it is exactly the place we are called to go in order to get to our idea of heaven ON EARTH and in the earth of our bodies and minds. Going into the fire, and the darkness saves your life and the life of your seed, because the darkness is where you learn to find your strength. In the wilderness of the darkness is where you are taught by your ancient guides to hone your skills to slay the inactivated dragons in others that attempt to come for you and yours. So, chosen ones, fear not going into the wilderness into which you are being called, because sometimes it is absolutely necessary to save whatever it is you were destined to bring forth into this world.

Once you know you are one of the chosen ones and have answered the calling within, you no longer worry about or fear the red (inactivated dragons) in other people, or worry about what others will think or say about you. Instead, you fear, become depressed, and are anxious about the consequences if you don't complete your born-with-it purpose and mission. That fear for me means, returning to this planet, to yet again cycle through karmic ties, ancestral trauma, childhood and sexual trauma, healing generational curses, falling into hell only to work my ass off to rise again. And I AM NOT COMING BACK TO DO THIS SHIT AGAIN! It's exhausting!

When you come into your ancient knowledge about yourself and your individual missions, when you decide to come back to the surface with your newly discovered diamonds and gold to share with the world, many will call you crazy as hell. They will say that you have lost your mind to think you could bring forth what you have been called to do, and they will be correct! Correct only in the fact that you purposely chose to go into your inner hell, gather your suppressed and hidden treasures, and rise back to the surface having lost your DAMN mind in the process. Yes, this makes you crazy as hell ***literally***—crazy as the hell you journeyed through to gain the insight you were called to bring to the world! Losing your mind is indicative of losing all the old beliefs and constructs that kept your power hidden; so, yes, you lost your mind so that you could gain a new one, and, yes, you are crazy as hell, because hell is exactly where you journeyed to go get your shit!

CONTEMPLATE SUICIDE OR HAVE THOUGHTS DEATH (SUICIDAL IDEATION)

The DSM-5 categorizes one of the criteria of depression as, the recurrent thoughts of death, *recurrent suicidal ideation* without a specific plan or a suicide attempt or a specific plan for committing suicide.

Activate

When I read this criterion the question for me became, are suicidal thoughts normal on this journey for the chosen ones?

And the answer is, HELL YES! Unless you take the journey through the darkness of your own mental disorder, independent of the complete dependence upon clinical or medical validation, you will ***misinterpret*** (such as traditional approaches already have*)* what it means to have suicidal thoughts at all! However, based on what we now understand, innerstand, and overstand according to the philosophies shared in this written work. Let's set new perimeters on exactly how you want to die. It is time to open your mind on setting the standards on a *new kind* of death.

When you take the journey through the darkness of your own mind regarding the contemplation of suicide, you are introduced to an alternate voice of your own. A voice that shares its ancient wisdom with you about your desire to die. For deeper insight, here is the first conversation I had with my "other voice" in the dark, on the evening I decided to die;

Me: Oh God, oh God, oh God, I don't know what to do, and everyone I thought was for me has turned their backs! Am I cursed or being punished for something? What is happening to me ... my life!?

The Voice: You're dying.

Me: Please don't let this be how I die, not like this! I don't deserve this, please help me!

The Voice: Yes you do deserve this.

Me: I do?

Voice: Yes! You deserve to die, because everything you think you are ... you are not. What you think you are must go! This death is necessary if you want to live.

Me: If I'm dying then how can I live?

The Voice: You will be reborn. You will emerge after death like a Phoenix rising from the ashes, but first you must die.

(**personal note:** *as I write this portion I become emotional. I pause for a moment to close my eyes before I can even continue. I reflect back on my journey through the dark.*)

Me: (reciting what felt like my last prayer) Yay, though I walk through the valley of the shadow of death, I will fear no evil . . ."

The Voice: And so it begins . . .

Now let's keep in mind that death is synonymous with *transition*, *changes*, and *shifting* from one state to another. Therefore, let's shift from thinking that death only exists in the physical form to one that allows you to die multiple times. Think about it, we have endured many deaths throughout our lives, haven't we? Deaths of unhealthy relationships, jobs, commitments, etc. Well, think of the thoughts of death on this journey as the deaths of the *old ideas*, *traditions*, *beliefs*, and ways of being and doing things that can no longer exist on your new journey. This kind of death, is where you get to raise yourself from the dead.

This journey through the darkness of mental disorder is *a type* of suicide that you don't have to make funeral arrangements for. Instead, it's a death of the masks you've been wearing your entire life! If you heed the perspectives that follow, you will rejoice about the suicidal thoughts you are having. Why? Because on this journey you get to choose which parts of you must die and which parts remain for your power to live and thrive. Although this may seem like a long stretch now, you and those who love and support you will celebrate your new ideas about death, trust! You will have the power with this new information to be wildly transformed, without a casket. Now, as

Activate

I mentioned before, if you decide to opt in for a casket, it will be because you are choosing to bury all of the shit you once thought about yourself, and thus will choose to have a traditional ceremony that symbolizes your newfound freedom. If so, make sure I get an invitation to sit right next to you on the front row, and we will smile together knowing that this is the moment of your metaphorical death and rebirth.

This journey is only for those of you who have taught yourselves how to hide your powers underneath trauma and pain. Disguising your natural born-with-it *talents*, *skills*, *dreams*, *visions*, *empathic abilities*, *spiritual gifts*, *psychic knowledge, and more*. You experience extreme levels of depression and anxiety, because there is an immense amount of ancient wisdom and gifts of power that has been suppressed and hidden away within you for centuries. You feel the strong effects of disorder's discomfort only because there may have been many lifetimes that you have hidden yourself, and now your power over time has grown exponentially. This power that lives beneath disorder and trauma, literally grew up as you grew up. As you aged and matured, all that you have kept suppressed has also aged and matured within you, causing discomfort. Imagine being held in the same size cage all of your life, and although you are growing, the cage stays the same size. Your anxiety and depression are like caged animals, waiting to burst loose and run wild! Anxiety and depression show up to say, there is no more room in the places you have stashed your power. LET ME OUT!

Remember in the chapter on **Mental Disorder and the Alchemical Process** where I discussed the concept of the fall? Well let's continue to dissect this idea of the fall. As previously discussed, I mentioned the idea of going down into the underworld of you and accessing your suppressed dark God/Goddess, Devil, Demon, and/or Savage that is showing up as anxiety, depression, and suicidal thoughts. We have always heard of the act of facing your inner demons, but what about the act of truly integrating your demons as an act of mental and emotional health? What about the idea of forging a relationship with the devil instead of vilifying this energy, so as to regain all of who and what you are contrary to what you've been taught about avoiding this so-called, "Lucifer"?

> **"This is the journey where you literally must descend down into your underworld and talk to the devil and demons to gain mental health and stability, and refine emotional intelligence."**
>
> **Timmésha Burgess**

Lucifer is defined as the planet Venus when it rises in the morning, a match struck by rubbing it on a rough surface, and according to *Wikipedia* in Roman folklore, Lucifer is defined as **"light-bringer"**; in Latin it was often personified as a male figure bearing a torch. Also, previously I mentioned that darkness is its own kind of light. Wouldn't this align with the notion of "light-bringer"? I sure think so! So, let's just consider the idea of a man carrying a torch, the wisdom that is activated within me says that this image symbolizes the "human carrying his fire," i.e., the Phoenix Fire bubbling underneath the surface of each and every one of us, awaiting our alchemical activation. As it relates to the Venus when it rises and a match when struck by rubbing it on a rough surface, I smile in the knowing that Venus represents the feminine rising, and a struck match against the rough surface is symbolic of the journey of the chosen ones . . . when we hit the roughness of rock bottom. How our journey to activating and unleashing out superpower had to be rough in order to wake us the Fuck up!

So, when you descend down into your inner hell, you get the amazing opportunity to meet "***El Diablo***" or "***La Diabla***," the part of you that you were taught to keep hidden away in your underworld for far too long. As mentioned in previous chapters, the work is to raise your inner dark self for activation to get the most out of all you are, and for the world and those around you to also benefit from you having done the work to integrate both your dark and light. To do this though, you must die. How else will you meet God or the Devil unless you die, right? I mean, the notion goes that when you die you either go to heaven or hell. Well, what if I told you that in this journey, that you go to both. As the alchemical process describes the act of first descending and then ascending again. Remember, this death is METAPHORICAL, of course. I cannot emphasize this enough. I want no one's family or friends coming after me saying I told anyone to literally kill themselves. But if you have gotten this far in this book, then that bit of common sense goes without saying for those of you on this journey.

So, I want to reiterate a point that I made in earlier chapters about the allegorical story of angels being kicked out of heaven onto earth. Remember when I mentioned earth being synonymous with our body in the seven (7) stages of seed-power growth? Well, to dive deeper into this aspect as it relates to suicidal thoughts, I am going to once again allow my ancient wisdom to be activated within me to speak to you. As usual, I can only share this idea with you as it is given to me.

Downloaded/Uploaded/ Intuitively Channeled Message

If there were angels kicked out of heaven onto earth, then wouldn't this make you those angels or the descendants of them? YES! What makes you think that you are not them and they are not you when you too are here on the earth realm, and when you too have descended and continue to do so until you wake up to who and what you are. What makes you think you are separate from them? You are the angels that were not thrown out of heaven (the heaven of you, i.e., your higher mind), but you are the angels that fell (descended) down into your underworld (lower-self) on purpose. You fall and rise over and over again to regain the knowledge of integration because it is imperative that you begin to forge a relationship between your God and Devil, your angel and demon. You must not be so heavenly bound that you are no earthly good and vice versa. Demons are also angels only hidden in darkness. They are not hiding there on their own, but you have hid them yourselves having been taught to do so through indoctrinated false teachings. You must learn how to raise your Devil to rule alongside God, and your demons (angels in the shadows) to rule alongside your light angels. This is where the awakening of your superpowers begin to alchemize and where you begin to regain and put back in order all parts of your mind and emotions that are out of order, thus developing your mental health. If you truly desire to regain your mental and emotional stability, the work lies in the inner alchemical process of rising, integrating, and inviting the Devil and demons to the table of you. You cannot have one without the other. The concept of God cannot exist without the Devil and the concept of Devil cannot exist without God. Therefore to shun the Devil and demon is essentially to engineer your own demise, and set the ground for the cause of your mental and emotional instability. It is like trying to have day without night; and it is like accepting the sun but spitting at the moon. God has never wanted to be without Goddess and without Devil. Humans' unhealthy egos and plans to gain and maintain rulership over others tore them apart. The light has never wanted to exist without the dark, the day has never wanted to exist without the night, and the sun has never wanted to exist without the moon.

There has never been a war against dark and light' it was the deactivated human's unhealthy ego that is responsible for fabricating a war between two infinite parts of the same whole—a fallacy that has placed a wedge between the polarities of God in and of itself; thus teaching you to war within yourself. Deactivated humans' unhealthy egos are the culprits that threw the rock, placing their hands behind their backs only to say that the darkness did it to the light! LIE!

Religious doctrine of false beliefs has taught you for centuries that there has always been a war between dark and light. And that the light would always prevail over the darkness; THIS IS A LIE! Dark and light exist equally and always will as infinite parts of polarity. You have and will always be fighting a NEVERENDING MAKE-BELIEVE WAR IN YOUR OWN MINDS in your attempt to defeat, hide, demonize, and vilify what has always and will always exist.

Your belief that light is greater than dark has taught those of you who appear darker on the surface of your flesh costume, to fear and hate yourselves and others that are of the same complexion. In-fact, this lie has taught you to hate and fear all things that are dark in nature such as, *black cats*, the "concept" of *black magic* (which as explained before, there is no such thing, but there are inactivated humans playing around with the power of alchemy to harm instead of heal), and taught you to vilify the darker masculine by using phrases such as *blackmail* (i.e., black male).

This fallacy of a war between dark and light has essentially torn you apart in your mind, and in your body, thus, causing your own mental and emotional disorder—splitting (instead of integrating) you. As God was split from Goddess and Devil, as heaven was split from hell, and as light was split from dark, you were split from your shadow-self. Therefore, you fear your own dark and what you have been taught to hide there.

Furthermore, to disrespect the dark, and the concept of demons and Devil is to disrespect yourself and your ancient ancestors. Because you are them and they are you—*you are one in the same*. The only time you should attempt to put a demon and Devil in its place, is when the inactivated demon and Devil in others, which have refused to rise to be crowned, attempt to cause harm to you and your loved ones unjustly.

But know this, that as you do the inner work to raise your own Devil and demon to the crown to be crowned through the alchemical fires of activation, the activated demon and Devil in others will honor and respect you. Because they will know that you have been crowned. Instead of attempting to harm you, they will instead choose to stand with, fight, and protect you alongside God as one of their own, from any of their other kin that tries to kill, steal from, and destroy you.

> When you are truly ready to face these truths and raise up your superpowers for mental health and emotional intelligence you will say, "**Devil, Moon, Demons, Dark/Shadow, and Hell, forgive me for treating you the way that I have. Forgive me for dismissing you and shunning you away. Because I am now awakened to these hidden truths, I choose to invite you to join together within me in holy matrimony. I now join together my heaven and hell, my dark and light within; because what God has joined together, may nothing and no one tear asunder.**
> —**The All**

As strange as this may sound, suicidal thoughts for the chosen ones begin to show up as proof that it is time to metaphorically (figurative, allegorical, symbolic, imaginative) die to all of who you thought you were and were taught to fear, so that you may be reborn into who and what you truly are. Unfortunately, this perspective of suicidal ideation has not been truly explored or dissected until now. I suppose it could not be openly discussed until this point of human evolution, until those of us who have taken the journey decide to publicly uncover these "other hidden" truths ourselves.

"Get excited about death now that you know how to die. Give your old false self and beliefs a proper burial! Cremate her, him, it in the flames of the alchemical fire. May they forever rest in peace."

Timmésha Burgess

Timmesha Burgess

As a chosen one you have survived the pressures of losing your mind, death threats, mockery, hate, slander, gossip, betrayal, heartbreak, frenemies, spell work, and past lives to get all of your shit back. Now that you have healed beyond generational curses, sexual trauma, being hung, burned, lied to, journeying into the underworld of hell, dying and being reborn to join together in holy matrimony your dark and light, angel and demon, sun and moon, yin and yang, God/Goddess and the Devil—it's a no brainer why anxiety, depression, and suicidal thoughts showed up not just in you, but FOR YOU! Showing up as proof that what you suffer from is not a sickness, but symptoms of suppressed spiritual gifts. Disorder in your mind and emotions is your proof that within you is a mistreated divine infinity that will no longer turn the other cheek, nor be hidden away in the shadows. This world and the world you are being guided to build is absolutely ready, waiting, needing, wanting, and desiring all that you have kept suppressed in the darkness of you. I, for one, cannot wait to see what you have kept hidden all this time.

Chapter 6: Lose Your Mind for Better Mental Health

> "No we're never gonna survive unless we get a little crazy."
> Singer/Songwriter Seal

How many times have you lost something, and simply decided to replace it?

What if I told you that you could do the same with your own mind? That you could lose your mind, and also replace it with an entire new one? Losing your mind indicates that you are ready to get rid of, do away with, and burn away all of the false beliefs you've been taught and held about yourself and the world around you. Losing your mind means that you no longer desire to identify with who and what societal expectations say you ought to be. Losing your mind means that you get rid of the old to make room for the new thoughts, new or uncovered ideas, beliefs, and ways of making decisions. Losing your mind to gain a new one is, hence, why the ideas I share here are considered unusual, weird, strange, and dark. These are the unorthodox perspectives that I gained, acquired, and earned when I took the journey through the uncharted darkness of disorder within myself—all of which I have been called to bring to light, to the world, and to you who is reading this book now.

As mentioned in the previous chapters, mental disorder simply means that there is a (dis)order of disseminated information in your mind and body. Anxiety, depression, and suicidal thoughts show up when it is time to properly redefine, organize, demystify, and unleash this trapped knowledge.

To realize that these "so-called" mental disorders are actually your power, you must not solely rely on modern medical studies, prescribed medications to pacify what is ready to wake up within you. I mean you can, but how has that worked out for those of you who have found yourself relying on therapy for years, dependent upon medications, and spending thousands of dollars on what you can already feel is a calling on a deeper, much darker level? Remember, that this body of work is designed for those of you who have been taught to believe that your symptoms of suicidal thoughts, anxiety, and depression are signs of mental disorder. **Activate** is developed as a tool for you to now move beyond diagnosis; because what you thought may have been disorder is truly your suppressed superpower of spiritual gifts, empathic abilities, clairvoyance, psychic knowledge, intuitive insights, dreams, visions, and DNA-coded ancient wisdom and intelligence banging at the doors within.

Although we love the work our counselors and therapists have attempted to do to support those struggling with and through what has been deemed as mental disorders, it's not enough for those of you on this particular journey of uncovering who and what you really are that may have been showing up as disorder all of your life. We have to go deeper, but unfortunately, traditional approaches steer clear of this type of depth. Why? Because not everyone is led to take such deep dives into the darkness of mental health and disorder. Only a few are called to first journey through it themselves—only to emerge with the wisdom required to guide others through it. Some licensed therapists work under a certain code of conduct to remain completely "neutral." However, there have been some who have followed an unorthodox way and were shunned for doing so. Yet, their clients were able to set themselves free in ways that others may have frowned upon. I don't mean in such ways as committing horrible acts against others and calling it "the purge"! Let's use our common sense here. My question has always been, how can anyone serve someone that dwells within the darkness of their mind, if they haven't, are too afraid to, or are "professionally" not allowed to enter the darkness themselves. This journey is for those of us that have walked through the "shadow of death," many deaths ourselves in fact, and have made it out alive only after having died. Those of us that have actually journeyed through the *internal conflict* (better known as hell) and lived to not only talk about it but also to teach others how to survive, thrive, and rise through and from it. I always say, "**How can anyone tell me how to get through hell if they've never been there?**"

It's time to take a dual approach to answering the questions your therapist just isn't equipped to handle. The content of this manual is tailored and targeted to teach you how-to laugh at the darkness of depression, smile at the moment of fear, and get excited at the rush of anxiety. This is your first step into the shadows of who and what you really are.

For a visual reference, let's think about divers that have attempted to explore uncharted territories of our oceans. Do you know that certain depths of our oceans have never been explored due to the amount of pressure exerted on humans there? Now let's compare this with the depths into the dark, shadow murkiness of mental disorder. Those parts yet to be fully explored due to the amount of pressure (*i.e., pains, discomfort*) it takes to go there. There are very few who have dared to journey these dark corridors through the mind and emotions, because too (much like a diver) pressure ensues, and very few can take it. At this level of depth into the darkness, no light or tools are available to assist because the deeper divers attempt to go, they are forced to abandon all forms of man-made mechanisms (*procedure, process, system, operation, method, technique, workings, means, channels, vehicle, structure*). Much like the experience of divers, for those that take the journey through the darkness of mental health, you are forced to go at it alone, leaving behind some if not ALL of the man-made mechanisms that first formed your mind. Forced to abandon any and all *outwardly* tools to help guide you other than your own inner-mechanism activated from within. This journey forces you to develop your own naturally born-with-it internal senses to help navigate you through, up, and out. This can be very scary, why? Because for centuries, you and those that came before you (ancestors) have been taught to vilify and sweep your abilities under the rug. Journeying through the darkness of mental disorder requires you to be led by what you cannot see. This is what it means when I say, "***When you feel you cannot see, and until you develop your ability to see in the dark... feel your way through.***"

Some dare to take this journey into the depths but turn back because they are not able to rely on their inner-mechanisms, or avoid this path altogether due to their fear of the dark. Some may have taken this path, but lose their minds in the process because they were not privy to the idea of gaining a new mind. Losing your mind is a powerful fucking thing and is actually the goal when you know what it means to lose it and go crazy in the first place. The kicker is: if you forget to gain a new mind after losing your old one in these uncharted inner waters, then *you will* without a doubt remain stuck in the abyss of your own darkness.

Louise Hay and Mona Schulz in their work titled **Heal Your Mind**,

> I have yet to meet anyone who was a shaman or an intuitive healer or a mystic of sorts who didn't have a lot of emotional and physical health problems. When it comes to the mind, I've found that people who work in the field of intuition, myself included, are some of the most modest, most anxious, irritable, high-strung, blunt, and

passionate individuals I have ever met." (Schulz and Hay, 267).

Today's *Diagnostic Statistical Manual* (DSM or DSM-5), suggests that your symptoms match several criteria relating to mental disorders. However, traditional approaches failed to incorporate spiritual, energetic, and/or otherworldly perspectives relating to those of you on this particular journey of activating your suppressed powers.

"To me this [DSM] is a house of cards and you can take off one or two cards at the top or you can knock over the whole thing. I prefer knocking over the whole thing."

—Dr. Thomas Szasz, Professor of Psychiatry, Emeritus

So, I've created an Activated version of the DSM, called the **DSM-A** (The Diagnostic Statistical Manual- Activated); designed to help guide you on what anxiety, depression and suicidal thoughts are for your particular path through the darkness of your mind and emotions. This manual will serve as your roadmap that offers insight and new perspectives to suggest what each symptom of depression, anxiety, and suicidal thoughts means for those of you who are naturally a ***born-with-it*** healer, intuitive, mystic, empath, clairvoyant, clairaudient, psychic. This Activated manual explains in-the-dark ideas about why you fit the criteria of isolation, confusion, insomnia, sadness and other mental health diagnosis, and why each of these symptoms are not reasons to worry, but reasons to celebrate your unseen victory of a power you have yet to activate.

DIAGNOSTIC STATISTICAL MANUAL-ACTIVATED (DSM-A)

ANXIETY REDEFINED

Anxiety speaks, but what is it trying to tell you? According to the **National Institute of Mental Health (NIMH)**, anxiety disorders affect 18.1 percent of adults in the United States, that's approximately 40 million adults between the ages of 18 to 54. Anxiety is associated with three or more of the following seven symptoms

https://www.ncbi.nlm.nih.gov/books):

1. Restlessness or feeling keyed up or on edge
2. Being easily fatigued
3. Difficulty concentrating or mind going blank
4. Irritability
5. Muscle tension
6. Sleep disturbance (difficulty falling or staying asleep, or restless unsatisfying sleep)
7. Anxiety or worry about having panic attacks, social phobia

DSM-A. Anxiety redefined

1. Restlessness or feeling keyed up or on edge

Activated Philosophy: I love to describe your hidden and suppressed power like this. Have you ever watched a wrestling match with tag team partners, where one fighter is in the ring and the other is on the outside of the ropes waiting to be tagged in? Well, your suppressed superpower is your tag team partner that is fully amped or keyed up on the outside of the ring, with its hand out saying, TAG ME IN!

The feeling of restlessness you are experiencing (if you're on this unorthodox path to mental health) is the impatience of your power growing thinner as you continue to give it the back seat in your life. It is the side effect of your stored up energy with nowhere to go and nothing to do. What do you expect would happen with the act of continuously storing power that has no outlet? That's right! A massive explosion, system overload, system failure and/or even system shut down.

This on edge powerful you is an indication that you've played the overly humble, safe, hidden, and acceptable role long enough. Your power is much more dynamic than you have given it credit, and you have been taught about it throughout centuries. Your power is showing up as restlessness because it is done with being on the sidelines of your life. Your restlessness is your long-awaited power clawing at the doors within you. Now is the time to answer that calling of alchemical activation to set it free. Practice tagging your power in, based on the **seven (7) stages of seed-power growth.** Journey through the darkness of where you have kept your tag-team power-partner hidden, do the inner dark work, and allow yourself to be guided by your born-with-it intuition, ancestors, and the ancients ones to rise.

2. Being easily fatigued

Activated Philosophy. I know exactly what it feels like when you don't even have the energy to just be here—to pray, meditate, or to even get up off the floor after such a long journey of dying and being reborn. I remember lying on my living room floor one night in a fetus position, tears running down the side of my face, with several pieces of used paper towels next to me wishing I could just shrink myself small enough to become invisible. I was so tired of feeling defeated in almost every area of my life, and I was exhausted with the constant demands from my brain saying "***I was doing too much and that I wasn't doing enough.***" Have you ever felt like you were doing too much and too little all at the same time? This is where you truly began to lose it! When I say lose it, I mean lose your damn mind, so that by some stroke of divine intervention and a wish upon several stars, you would somehow gain a whole new mind. I realized that for me on the journey through the darkness of my mental health, I was tired as hell yes! Tired of the way my life seemed to have a default setting automatically gauged for "destruction" and/or "close but no cigar" at every turn—with mere fleeting moments of happiness. I was fatigued because it seemed like that when I took 10 steps in what seemed like the right direction, I was catapulted back 75 steps backward! After hitting my level of rock bottom (for the third or fourth time in my life), I decided to just lay on the rock for a moment to contemplate why the FUCK I was back down here again! After enough times of being on the hard bottom, I finally realized why I was truly tired. The fatigue was coming from the drain I felt from wearing the masks of trying to build a life on the faulty premises I had been taught and on which, in turn, I had taught myself. I was fatigued from the years of playing characters in a play for which I never even knew I had auditioned. Perhaps, you too are done with playing dress-up and are ready to burn away the costumes, open yourself to what has been hidden from the light of day. If this is the case, your fatigue is much more than just being tired from lack of energy; it means your true power is damn tired of not being properly activated by you and you alone. You also realize that the masks you have been wearing your entire life is the one that is actually feeling and causing the fatigue; it in turn is telling you that it is TIRED OF BEING YOUR FRONT MAN!

So I say, just lie on the rock bottom floor! Lie there and don't get up until the fatigue you feel *becomes* the exact fuel you need to stand up again. How does it become your fuel you wonder? You'll finally get tired of being tired! I'm sure you've heard of this one before, right? When you've been fatigued for so long that you become bored of it! But until you get to this place, don't fucking move! If you only decide to get up to get some water, then do so and lay your ass right back down on the rock-bottom floor. After a while of laying there, you'll soon decide that you're ready for a more comfortable setting. Then and only then will you gather the strength from the reserves of your power to allow you to simply stand and make the step toward your climb back to the top. But this time, you'll be using a whole new strategy to climb to heights you never even thought possible before. Moreover, fatigue sets in when your spiritual body becomes aware that you've been here before. Meaning, you come into the knowledge that this is your eleventh lifetime of coming to this planet to complete whatever missions you didn't fulfill in the previous lifetimes. Your spiritual body is the one that feels this tiredness, and you sometimes think it's your physical body. It is not. Your ancient soul remembers (put back together) the pieces of you from past lives that have been here and done this several times over. This is okay. Just know that your fatigue lies deeper in your soul, and the work to ease fatigue is to forge a lifestyle of ease, vacations, peace, and drama-free encounters. Steer clear of people, places, and things that exacerbate the MESS! You are here again to fulfill your purposeful missions, and because you are too tired to come here and do this shit again, get it done this lifetime.

3. Difficulty concentrating or mind going blank.

Activated Philosophy: If your mind goes blank often, well CONGRATU-FUCKIN-LATIONS! This means you have already accomplished the goal that all monks, the highly enlightened, and meditation gurus have been trying to reach and teach for centuries—the art of quieting the mind. HA! Seriously, think about it. We've all heard of that day ole' saying from meditation experts on quieting the mind, right? Well, if the mind is blank, didn't you achieve a point of galactical enlightenment? It is unfortunate that it's okay to accept a blank mind from peace experts, but vilify it in our day to day. Sure, this concept may seem whacky, but why not run with it if it works for you? So, what if the path to achieving a clear mind is wrapped in what "is called" anxiety; however, we've established early on what is called "anxiety" is suppressed superpower rumbling to be unleashed. Capitalize off this new information about what it means for your mind to go blank by using the times your mind decides to take hiatus to go within. Why not use your moments of "going blank" to achieve what masters have been trying to achieve since the dawn of time?

On my journey through the darkness of my mental health, I found that when my mind would go blank, it was an indication that something else wanted to speak from the shadows. A blank mind gives space for new ideas to rise up. So don't fight it! Now if you happen to be in conversation and your mind goes blank, it may also be an indication of channeling that wants to come through and your brain must shut off for your inner mind to speak up. On the other hand, it may also be that what was about to be said wasn't meant to be said at that time or place.

Allow the space in your mind to be there without trying to find a specific thought to grab hold of simply because someone taught you to be afraid of void.

Going blank when channeling

If you're reading this book, then you already have some awareness of what channeling is and means; if not then here is a quick definition.

> Channeling is the act of translating messages from another consciousness. In the spiritual field, this usually means translating messages from beings that exist outside of the 3D reality. A Channel is a person who has the ability to channel these beings. Their words

are often taken as the ultimate truth because they are coming from higher dimensions, but most people don't understand they have their own perspectives and therefore limitations of perspective as well.

Teal Swain, *International Speaker and Best-Selling Author*

On this journey, you realize that a side-effect to being able to interpret messages from the divine source—whether you call it God, Universe, Ancestors, Angels, Spirit guides or other—is your mind going blank. Divine source according to this written work is the integration of higher and lower realms together as one. When the marriage of God and Devil, light and dark, higher and lower happens within you, your power to channel heightens. Here's an example: You're in meditation (singing, dancing, skating, running, etc.) and all of a sudden, a thought or vision occurs that's so profound that you forget that you were even in the middle of a meditative activity at all. Have you ever had an idea come to you in the middle of a conversation and you forgot what you were talking about? This is it! This is when the idea of the blank mind is at its finest, and the most ripe time to home in on what is rising through the blankness or removal of the initial thought. We call it going blank because the initial thought is removed, but what we have not been taught to home in on is the new thought coming through—even if you have to tell the person you were speaking with to hold for one sec while you jot down a quick note. If they are of your like-minded tribe, they'll surely understand, innerstand, and overstand.

4. Irritability

Activated Philosophy: On this journey through the dark of your mind, irritability sets in for a plethora of reasons. Below I highlight main two **(2) main** reasons why irritability will set in for those of you on this unique path to activation; some of which may align with your journey:

- *Family telling you what they think you should or should not do.*

    When another source of power speaks from within you, this voice is independent of everyone's else's opinion if it means the silence of it. You will wish you did not become so irritated at the opinions of those who you know love you, but you will. Why? Because their views may not align with your individual calling, and your emotions will feel annoyed at their audacity. However, your love for them and theirs for you will hopefully help smooth the rough road of your powers coming online. When you fully come into your power and purpose, they and you will have understood what it was all for. If and when irritation grows stronger, it is time to step away from even the ones you love, because irritation can harm them and others, but you are for the first time awakening raw power. Refer to the **seven (7) stages of seed-power growth** for reference as often as you need so that you can practice. Raising your fires will elicit irritation because it is rising from the lower self (root, sacral chakras), which are responsible for these emotions, but remember the work is to refine your emotions for intelligence, and realizing that when irritation sets in, this is because the work you are doing to rise or the work you have not yet done to refine. Either way, be sure to communicate your needs, and remove yourself when needed to protect yourself and others.

- **CONSTIPATION**

    Straight up! Although seemingly an ignored point to discuss on the basis of mental health, this is HUGELY crucial as you journey through the darkness of your mind and your body. Do the research on the symptoms of constipation, and you'll be floored to learn that irritation is the main symptom of constipation. I'm going to be really honest here, I struggled with constipation from my undergraduate days and never really took it seriously until I couldn't lose weight, and my skin started to break out! How upsettingly funny would it be for you to discover that what you think is anxiety is really the cause of a colon full of shit! HA! I'm laughing hard as I write this, but unspoken truths are still truths! Would your traditional clinical therapist suggest for you to detox your body as a way to unleash your trapped power showing up as anxiety? NOT LIKELY! We talk so much about detoxing our lives of toxic people, friends, relationships, narcissistic family members, jobs, and habits as a means to ensure our safety and overall well-being, but let's not forget our bodies as it relates to mental health, too.

On my journey, I found that although I was doing the work from within to unleash my power, it meant nothing if my body was just going to hold onto the same exact stuff I was trying to clear. What's the point of activating power you can't even use because there's stuff blocking its path? You'll read more on how my appetite shifted in the depression chapter, but I want to point out that I invested in my body from within. I didn't just burn sage, hold crystals, and chant! I may have had only a few dollars to my name during this time, but I still chose to invest in my health instead of eating fast food. I took the little money I had and purchased sea moss, alkaline foods, and natural herbs. For anyone that knows the herbal world, you'd know these investments aren't cheap. I knew that by spending the little money I did have on detoxing would keep me from buying into eating habits that further perpetuated blocked energy in me. I was over it! Even if that meant not eating so that I could set myself free, I chose it, why? Because I knew there would be no way I could fully unleash my trapped power if I did not. It was a matter of life and death as it relates to my life's mission to uncover this thing we call anxiety. I refused to allow my body to stand in the way of the new "body" that was ready to be born.

I'm not a licensed physician so I can't give you any medical advice, but I say seek all the above. Seek a medical opinion, seek out health gurus, and ask your doctor yourself. If you haven't already, do your due diligence and dig deep into holistic systems and practices that clear and detox the body of stuck and stagnant detritus. Not just poop, but old and stuck energy PERIOD. Walk through the darkness of your mind and body, not just to clear traumas learned, but also traumatic energies that literally attach themselves to your colon, spleen, mind, lungs, heart, etc. Think of it as a grand kickstart to turning your pain into power.

5. Muscle tension

Activated Philosophy: On my journey I found that muscle tension was due to two things:

- From being in spiritual battle
- Stuck, blocked, and stagnant energy

I remember having a conversation with my middle sister one day walking to brunch one morning when she said, "*I just realized that I sleep with my hands balled.*" I told her that I found that out about myself a couple of years prior, and that our brother William does the same thing, and why? Because when you've been through hell, YOU ARE TENSE. I can think about soldiers who have come home from war, and are shell shocked from the trauma they endure with having to watch their backs 24/7. It is the same for those of us who have been on the journey of our lives. When you are in battle or just come out of war, you are tense as hell! Why? Because hell is where you've just come from. Listen, it's so perfect when you know this because now you can do the work to tell your body, "*Listen you made it through and out. It's okay now. I've got you.*"

As it relates to stuck energy, well this is what this entire written work is about isn't it? Muscle tension can stem from holding on to energy that is supposed to be flowing through and out of the body. Refer to the **seven (7) stages of seed-power growth** again and again for more insight.

6. Sleep disturbance (difficulty falling or staying asleep, or restless unsatisfying sleep).

Activated Philosophy: Remember in number one above where we talked about your energy being keyed up because it's been either inactivated, misused, and abused so long that it's over it and ready to be properly inactivated by you and only you. Meaning it's ready to be tagged in? On this journey your sleep patterns are going to be all screwed up, they just are! Now this doesn't mean we never sleep again, but you quickly learn the reason so many greats who have created great things on this planet say things like, "I'll sleep when I'm dead." I get it! As an empathic, one your abilities is to be so charged that sleeping will almost seem irrelevant (although contrary to popular opinion) due to the fact that you'll be much too amped about what you're being called to create. You'll find yourself getting up out of bed to write down a vision, epiphanies, and channeled or inactivated messages that may decide to awaken within you in the middle of the night or wee hours of the morning. As you begin to activate your born-with-it gifts and superpowers, you will not be able to sleep most nights because you will be called to pray, meditate, write, dance, or simply just sit outside and stare at the moon. Why the moon? Because mama moon may be beckoning you for communion; especially if there's a full moon or one approaching. Don't fight yourself on not being able to sleep. Instead, on these nights, simply tune into what is coming through you, write it down or use a voice recorder, draw it out, and then if you decide, go ahead and lay back down. You may find that after you've gotten out of bed to do this, you will naturally fall off to sleep. Why? Because what needed to come through and out of you did, and is no longer trapped within trying to speak. You have given it room to come up and come out, and for this tell yourself, "Thank you!"

7. Worry about having panic attacks, panic disorder, negative evaluation in social anxiety [social phobia].

Activated Philosophy: This is my favorite one of the seven. Why? Because you get to truly demystify the bull-crap of this so-called criteria. Let me tell you something! When you have survived current and past lives, death threats (or even been murdered in past lives), spell work meant to kill, stealing from meant to destroy you, hate, sabotage, mockery, slander, abuse, sexual trauma, being hanged or burned, accused of being wicked to you all because you can feel, see, and know things on deeper levels, and left for dead by those closest to you—why would you not exhibit discomfort when in social setting?

I mean when I first experienced a panic attack, I was at a public event with hundreds of people. At that time I was beginning to forge a relationship with two guys from a magazine company that I thought were trustworthy. I later found out that they were social predators and were out for the strangest act of bloodsucking I had ever seen before. One guy's aim the entire time was to gain my ideas and use them as his own, and the other guy's motive was to sleep with me. My panic attack showed up like a SIREN, to say, get the hell away and from around these guys because they are not for you!

For those of you on this path, think of social phobia as your body responding to either current or past trauma, because if there's one thing I've learned on this path through the darkness of my mind and emotions; is that if and when you are around those that are truly your tribe, your intelligent self will have no need to press the panic button. Contrary to what others may say about this concept, even if there is no one around actually coming at you with a knife, your energy will feel into what you cannot see, especially when it's been raised through alchemical activation. Your energy will warn you through panic attacks that this may not be the room for you or your people. Do not confuse nervousness with panic attacks; nervousness says "***Wow I'm doing something I've never done before and I'm excited about it.***" A panic attack says, "***Something is definitely wrong up in here! And although I can't see it, something in me can feel it.***"

Depression Redefined

According to the Diagnostic and Statistical Manual of Mental Health Disorders, depression is defined as:

Depression DSM-5 Diagnostic Criteria

The DSM-5 outlines the following criterion to make a diagnosis of depression. The individual must be experiencing five or more symptoms during the same two-week period and at least one of the symptoms should be either (1) depressed mood or (2) loss of interest or pleasure.

1. Markedly diminished interest or pleasure in all, or almost all, activities most of the day, nearly every day.
2. Significant weight loss when not dieting or weight gain, or decrease or increase in appetite nearly every day.
3. A slowing down of thought and a reduction of physical movement (observable by others, not merely subjective feelings of restlessness or being slowed down).
4. Fatigue or loss of energy nearly every day.
5. Feelings of worthlessness or excessive or inappropriate guilt nearly every day.
6. Diminished ability to think or concentrate, or indecisiveness, nearly every day.

Depression redefined- The *Activate* Unorthodox Criteria

1. **Markedly diminished interest or pleasure in all, or almost all, activities most of the day, nearly every day.**

Activated Philosophy: So, all of a sudden or over time you've STOPPED being interested in the things you used to love. On this unorthodox journey, you are no longer interested in the usual activities, because something much more powerful within you realizes that the day to day, same-old things are fleeting. In the words of Belle from *Beauty and the Beast*, "**There must be more than this provincial life!**" YOU GOT THAT RIGHT, BELLE! I could no longer find (even if I wanted to) a good enough reason to be interested in the things that hoarded my attention before. I realized that my lack of interest was due to a much deeper calling for satisfaction.

You see, this much more powerful you that lives within is bored with activities that don't speak to its much more profound missions. For example, you've always participated in going for drinks on the weekends with friends, colleagues, etc. and now your response is, "Maybe some other time." They assume something's wrong with you or that you're blowing them off when really, you're just done with doing the same old shit! I uncovered a monumental truth that my disinterest in most activities was an indication that I was over simple-minded experiences and people. There were "certain people" in my life that I later found to be part of the reason I was experiencing pain and betrayal repeatedly—from frenemies to toxic relationships, jobs, and even toxic family members. This shift led me to the core of myself to discover that not only was I done with certain activities, but that I was also done with certain people.

Non-action is a powerful freaking tool once you know ***how to be*** inactive. When you pull away from mundane daily activities, you discover that there is something else much more active that exists *within* you during non-activity. A you that's been waiting for *you* to sit still long enough to focus on it. And the only way that "this" you can get your attention is through the strong pull of depression. Non-activity helps you to tune into the hidden you, so that you can not only ask questions, but receive the answers from and through yourself.

- Communication is key on this journey through the darkness of mental health; even if what you say is foreign to whom you're addressing. Speak up by boldly saying, "**I choose not to do (fill in the blank) simply because it no longer interests me. I am in a space where I am figuring out what I want to do, why I want to do it, and with whom. I need and am taking this time to do that alone. Thank you for understanding** (*even if they don't understand, say it anyway*); **I will be in touch.**"

- Continue to remain in your space of inactivity until further notice. After a while of continuously choosing not to hang out, some family members and friends will start to question if you're okay. They will wonder why you no longer participate in traditional gatherings. To be quite frank, once you've come to terms with who and what you are because you're now activating this inner power that's awakening itself in you, you may just decide not to get back in touch at all with some of your old friends and family. The great thing is, in your space of solitude (non-activity), you will without a doubt have full clarity about who gets to stay, and who absolutely MUST GO!

As I began to come into the hidden truths about what I was pressing down ("de" pressing) that was showing up as a lack of interest in my usual day to day activities with myself and with others, I QUIT THE WORLD COLD TURKEY! I lacked interest in the mundane because for so long I was masking something within me that was ready to explode, and the only way that I could get to know this "something" for myself—without the input from the world—was if I pulled completely back from the day-to-day bullshit. Once I began to do the inner work to uncover what this symptom of depression was for me, I knew that it would be much longer before I was actively involved in anything outside of myself again. Why? Because this profound something that was beginning to rise within me, needed my *full attention* and to be fully protected from outside opinions, judgments, and even attacks from spell work as mentioned in previous chapters.

2. Significant weight loss when not dieting or weight gain, or decrease or increase in appetite nearly every day.

Activated Philosophy:

> When individuals are not recognizing that it is the mind and the emotions that determine the contour, the shape, the actual action of the physical body, they think that they don't actually have to speak about what they're thinking and feeling and nobody will know.... Whatever you are thinking and whatever you feel is determined and exhibited by your physical body. So when you are excess in emotional waste, oh yes you are going to be overweight.
>
> **Dr. Jewel Pookrum**

For this (de)pressed, hidden you to speak, it has to have a clear channel to do so. Therefore, your body responds by a change in appetite. You may no longer crave or be satisfied by certain foods because this more powerful you is ready to come through. It can only do so when the channels (your body) are clear enough for it to do so. The magic though is not getting stuck in the *in-between* of your body *shifting* gears. The weight loss could be a side-effect to your body clearing itself of energy that no longer serves it. Also, the weight loss could be due to no longer eating what you used to eat, such as certain sugars, meats, dairy, etc., because this inactivated you will command higher vibrational foods; so don't be alarmed. Instead, pay attention to what information comes through you such as thoughts, ideas, visions, promptings. This is the prime time to listen to the inner you, because your body is becoming clear of blockages. As you do the work to activate, your body will naturally begin to trim because any energies that were once stuck and stagnant are clearing out.

Once I delved into the dark of this internal exploration, I innerstood that I needed to allow my body to purify itself through this transition in its own productive way. I tuned into why my appetite had shifted so drastically to the point that I would refuse to eat because I didn't feel like it. I paid attention to what my body was asking for. It wanted dark green leafy things, plain spicy jalapenos (I would literally bite into a raw jalapeno), and I'd bite into whole, raw white onions. Yes my body required it! Needless to say, I didn't do any dating during this time, HA! My body craved fruit and kale smoothies, spicy soups, and warm teas. Now don't get me wrong, I did not and will NOT EVER give up chocolate, no way. But I did allow my body to speak, and I listened to a language that I had previously taught myself to ignore. Then all of a sudden, I got up one day and said, "*If I for some reason can't get my hands on the foods my body is asking for, then I won't eat at all until I do.*" However, if your body seems to be telling you that it is craving alcohol, candy, and cake all day. Then it's time for you to do the research on specific detox and nutrition programs and seek out a medical physician or specialist to find out why.

Because I allowed myself to tune in to what was going on inside of me, I was able to feel a sense of ease. I was internally being led to facts and truths that just could not be Googled. I became amazed at what was happening on a deeper level. On the levels of normative science and medicine, this could not be explained with logic, blood tests, graphs, and charts. I was led to discover for myself that there was an *insurmountable* reservoir of thoughts, ideas, dreams, and visions that I kept trapped inside of not only my mind but also in my body, with nowhere to escape. My body was literally telling on me, but to me!

As it relates to weight gain:

When there is stuck, stagnant energy (i.e., excess emotional waste), the body will most definitely hold on to weight in the form of adipose tissue, bloat, water gain, etc. Moreover, an increase in appetite on this journey may be a clear indication of your body wanting more of the foods that help it to **thrive**. This does not mean eating anything and everything. It may signify that yes it wants more food, but more of the foods that give it what it needs to properly activate and transmute energy. When we hold on to trauma, weight is sure to accumulate. Not only did my body seem to puff up at different levels of my journey, but so did my face! It would seem that one week my body appeared in range, and then the next it was as if someone blew air into me OVERNIGHT! My face would look as if I had been kissed by a puffer fish, and my stomach bloated and bulged as if I was pregnant. I knew on a deep level that the shifts happening with my body were the result of a pushing and pulling of something much more profound happening within. And that this something had no real direction in which it could, should, or would go, until I discovered that my body as the vessel/vehicle was missing its captain—ME!

So one day, I looked at myself in my bathroom mirror. I mean I really looked into my eyes, I opened my mouth and looked as far back into my throat as I could, at my lips, my ears, and my barely-there eyebrows. I studied my body outwardly so that I could get a sense of what was happening inwardly. I cried deeply and words I had never spoken out loud poured out from my stomach and from my chest. I spoke in ways I had never heard myself speak before, words that affirmed to me who I was, what I am, and what was sure to happen next. All of which I am going to share with you here.

For unexplained weight gain: "Body, I know that you are holding on to this energetic weight because of the sexual trauma you experienced as a child, and for any other reasons you may have felt pain. I know this weight has shown up as a form of a protection or barrier with the goal of safeguarding my body from harm. I know that this weight has only shown up as a way to protect me. This extra weight has come because my body felt that I needed an extra layer of protection, and I appreciate, you body, for doing your best to protect me. Thank you for doing your best to protect me from any and all forces that attempt or have attempted to harm me. You have done well extra weight/fat, you have served your purpose. But now I choose to release you because I no longer require your services. I love you, and thank you."

For weight loss when not dieting: "Body, I know that you are purging all those things within me that are not equipped to sustain the high power trying to work its way through me! I understand that you are clearing out the old to make room for the new, So I allow it! Thank you, body, for getting rid of all the old, stuck, and stagnant energy that has kept me and my power trapped. I am thankful for this purge, because I know that it is necessary for me to be clear about what my body requires for me to function optimally. I know you are merely responding in a way to suggest that it's time for a change. Thank you, body, for purging out what no longer serves me and keeps me heavy or weighed down. I know that we need to have optimally functioning health to do the work we've been called to do. Thank you for teaching me how to let go of the old that no longer serves me. I realize that you are releasing the old energies in my body to make room for the incoming new, the better, and the greater to enter me now. And so it is."

A slowing down of thought and a reduction of physical movement (observable by others, not merely subjective feelings of restlessness or being slowed down).

Activated Philosophy: On this journey through the darkness of your mind and emotions, you must slow down your thinking because thinking will get in the way of your intuitive abilities. There's no need for thinking because the only thing your brain is capable of at this point is attempting to think based on the former perimeters set for it by a world that no longer exists for you. So your brain cannot help you with its thinking. Remember the example of the deep divers and how they have to abandon all forms of previous equipment when diving to certain depths? Well, your slowing down of thought and reduction of physical movement is the abandonment of all your former thoughts that can no longer serve you where you are going. You'll need your inner intuition for this. You might as well hang a sign on your head that reads, "NO THINKING ALOUD UNTIL FURTHER NOTICE FROM MY SPIRIT GUIDES."

As I write this portion, I am seeing a vision of a soldier or an assassin in the wilderness, closing their eyes, slowing their breathing, and calming their mind. Why? Because they cannot rely on their brain to hit the target; they must activate their senses to tune in. I see a cold fog coming from their mouth, and I can hear slight breathing as hey inhale and exhale slowly. I can see movement through the trees. The soldier or assassin with their eyes remained closed feels/senses where the target is and its next move. They then aim and fires, and hits the target. BULLS EYE!

4. Fatigue or loss of energy nearly every day.

Activated Philosophy: Although we've already delved into this criterion under Anxiety Redefined, I feel we can go one more round. Since the original DMS likes to repeat itself, so will I.

On this journey through the darkness of your mind and emotions, fatigue seems to be a constant companion. It says "*I'm tired, but not sleepy.*" Yes, you are tired, but not from the usual causes of tiredness such as keeping up with a busy schedule and grueling tasks. This type of fatigue is from the lack of use of your **born-with-it** power. Fatigue or loss of energy for those of us on this journey isn't showing up as some mysterious component just because you are all of a sudden labeled as depressed. You can compare this to when you develop muscle atrophy from not using your muscles regularly, such as a lack of walking, standing, etc. This is synonymous with the type of fatigue and loss of energy you are experiencing now. Yet, it is proof that your power suffers from lack of use. So, you grow fatigued, and lose energy DAILY, meaning your power's energy remains without activation from you! But celebrate this ancient insight about why fatigue has shown up for you, because you now have been given the most powerful information about why this is your experience, what it is, and what to do about it. If you choose to do something about it, this is the time. It is time to call your power to the forefront.

Get a piece of paper and something to write with. I don't care if you write in your own blood (which may be best, just kidding); DO IT! Write down everything you think makes you tired in your day-to-day. You can become absolutely exhausted from thinking the same thoughts over and over on repeat, this is a fact! So, if it's thoughts that you feel brings on more fatigue, write these thoughts down, too.

Read each line then say out loud, "I choose to call my power to the forefront NOW so that it may energize me and bring me back into alignment with all parts of me once scattered, and torn apart!"

Take your paper and safely burn it (in a safe burning container).

Spread the ashes in a hole you dig yourself, release them in water, flush them, or let them blow away in the wind. Whichever option you choose, get rid of the ashes.

5. Feelings of worthlessness or excessive or inappropriate guilt nearly every day.

Activated Philosophy: In 2020, (the year in which we all recall the year "the world stopped"), the year our world shifted into the new age and gave rise to the true Phoenixes, I was invited to speak on a global platform. The event was called the "United Consciousness Conclave 2020," and it was broadcasted on six different continents. I was the only African-American woman to speak at this virtual event of 20 speakers from all parts of the world, where even His Holiness **"THE" Dalai Lama** sent his blessings! Master seekers and speakers gathered together from Argentina, India, France, Brazil, and Egypt, just to name a few countries, to share their ideas on consciousness. After my speech, I was invited to be a part of a panel discussion, during this Q & A I was asked my perspective on dealing with guilt. My response was simple, "Guilt is a seed that was planted by someone. Who was it and why?" When guilt comes up for you, the very first thing to do (as with anything) is question it. For those of us on this journey through the darkness of our mental health, what we perceive to be guilt is simply a seed that grew from us choosing to do what we wanted to do, contrary to traditions, family beliefs, religion, and social/societal expectations. Guilt can either be self-taught or forced onto us by outside influences, and it can even have karmic ties (family issues that travel though bloodlines). Yes there is such a thing as karmic ties, many of us know this as "generational curses." But do your own research on what this may look like for your particular journey before pointing the finger at your great great-great-grandma or -grandpa!

Guilt reared its head for me at excruciatingly deep levels due to my ideas about my lack of financial success and how I should have just gotten a 9-to-5 instead of trying to build a brand. I felt deep guilt that I was attempting to support women and girls by teaching them how to turn their pain, anxiety, and depression into their own power, when I still felt very powerless due to my financial circumstances. I was jobless, went from having my own home to needing financial support from family members, I could no longer manage payments on anything, and lost the life insurance I had been paying into since I was eighteen, and even as I write this book, I am living with my sister and sister in-law.

Why did I feel the emotion of guilt? Because I (on a material level) had no proof that I was successful at turning my own pain into my power until writing this book! I smile because I realize that my guilt came from comparing my worth and value to how much money I had. The guilt I felt was that I was writing a book on unorthodox philosophies about mental health while I was receiving unemployment (until it ran out) and food stamps.

How did I overcome my guilt?

I realized that I am the manifestation of infinite creation and did not need to apologize for creating anew. I owed no apologies for going through hell to uncover my true nature and the reason I exist on the planet. Guilt could no longer exist for me because I was not sorry about the fact that it had to be this way for me, and for so many on the path of death and rebirth. I owe no explanation for getting it all out of the mud myself. I had to redefine who and what I was based on what I had learned in the darkness of me. But before that, I had to unlearn societal expectations of who I thought I was supposed to be that was purely based on material accumulation. We always hear folks say, "*You are enough.*" But one day I asked myself, that in fighting in the battle of my life, if all I walked away with was myself, would that be enough? My answer: HELL, YES! All that I rediscovered within me during the darkest parts of my life, I found to be infinite, abundant, life-bringing, and UNFUCKWITHABLE! That is not just enough, but MORE THAN enough! In the battle of my life, I came out with all of my hidden treasures as my own personal spoils of war. What guilt could possibly exist in the truth that I am my own spoils of war?

I discovered that my treasures were my individual **value**, and that is my **power**, not money. And that for the rest of my life, money will work tirelessly to match and measure itself up to my rich, limitless, infinite and abundant value, not the other way around.

<blockquote>
"I redefine the meaning of power.

Value = Power."

Timmésha Burgess
</blockquote>

To solidify this point, I'd like to share what was told to me by my spirit guides;

> **Write this book despite the distractions and the fears you have about not having a job or lots of money, brighter days will come for you. Share with the world what we have taught you, and what you have learned in the dark about the darkness, and you will never want or worry about your stability, well-being, safety, peace, and life again. This is a promise.**

So, if you are on this journey, I suggest that you get a piece of paper and something to write with. If you have neither because you have just begun your descent into your underworld and are without, then write it in your own ***blood*** if you must! Just make sure you stay conscious long enough to read the rest of the manual. Don't bleed out! I want no lawsuits!

Write down everything you feel the *energy of guilt* about—be it persons, places, things, and experiences. Remember guilt is energy just like any other emotion, thing, or person. This book that you hold in your hand is pure energy made up of molecules vibrating so fast that they clump together forming a solid source. So just like this book in your hand, you get to hold the energy of guilt in your hand and then pour it all out on paper. Burn the paper safely while saying, "**Out with the old and in with the new. My powerful value, I now make room for you.**"

6.   Diminished ability to think or concentrate, or indecisiveness, nearly every day.

Activated Philosophy: We've also addressed this criterion under Anxiety, but again since the DSM likes to repeat itself, so will I. This is one of the most misunderstood components of depression that really boils me. Name one human on the planet who has never experienced indecisiveness or an inability to concentrate, and I'll show you a human that isn't actually human or even from planet earth. EVERY SINGLE PERSON experiences this, and since we know this to be fact, does this mean that every single human is depressed? The answer is yep!

You will no longer suffer in indecisiveness because your inactivated self intuitively knows where to go, what to do, what to say, how to say it, when to do it, and to whom. You will no longer be confused about who and what you are, and you will no longer suppress all that you were created to become and unbecome. Your indecisiveness is only due to fear of yourself, fear of fully showing the world all that you are because you were taught to hide in the dark so well. Once you do the inner alchemical work to integrate both your light and dark, angel and demon, heaven and hell, God/Goddess and Devil for mental health and emotional intelligence, your yin and yang will no longer be in conflict within you. All within you will work together in perfect harmony, to guide you on charting your own course and building your own new world. You will be the example that will teach others what it looks like to truly go through hell, only to rise through the ashes of the old like a Phoenix into your inner heaven. You will be the epitome of what it means to turn pain into power, and how to gain mental health through the activation of "hidden in the dark" superpower.

Activate

Timmesha Burgess

ACTIVATE GLOSSARY

Demons (noun): *Angels in disguise, dark angels. Ancient ancestors that live in the shadows.* They are what we call demons, and we are their offspring. Just like we are the descendants of our parents who gave birth to us. When emotional intelligence and mental health is gained with the philosophes shared in ***Activate***, you properly become a channel and vessel for our shadow ancient ancestors (demons) to rise up through. Ancients rising back up through us is not a new thing, it's a trapped thing. Over time, psychological tactics have and continue to be devised to stop and/or delay our ancestors from rising out of the shadows through us, because we have been taught to fear them. This keeps many of our ancient dark ancestors trapped in our inner hell.

Hell (noun): *The underworld, darkness, shadow, the womb and/or vagina, earth, down there, or over there, Yin, an equal counterpart to heaven. The dark side of the sun.* To enter heaven, we all must first enter into hell. In_*another sense,* heaven also exists in the underworld; hence the saying, "*Heaven's gates are between her leg*s."

Mental disorder (noun): *Stored energy not in its rightful place.* Power out of order, or disorganized in the body and mind.

Mental illness (noun): *Not the same as a mental disorder.* When a person *purposely* and *knowingly* chooses not to misuse and abuse to fuel toxicity. A sickness motivated by chaos and confusion in those who seek to cause harm to others, without probable cause. Usually treated with clinical trials and medications.

Savage/Beast/Devil (noun): *The hidden warrior.* The part of us that we've been taught to vilify. Our protector that takes no shit.

Activate

Timmesha Burgess

Acknowledgements

To my passed-on grandparents Lessie and Robert Burgess, ancestors, ancient ones, and spirit guides: Thank you, Grandma and Grandpa, for coming through to me when I cried out for you. I'm singing, *"Never would have made it without you,"* when I think of you. Thank you, ancestors and ancient ones, for trusting me with this knowledge and choosing me to bring it to the world.

To my sister Jessica: I'm singing Destiny's Child, *"You are my best friend, and you've been right there through thick and thin. You are my best friend, gotten me through places I've been. You are my best friend, through my situations, you've been my inspiration. My best friend, you're still here, and I love you."* My Jessica, all I can say is that if I got it, you got it, PERIOD! Thank you for having my back and allowing me the space to be **Dangerous**.

To my mommie: Thank you, Mom, for surviving your own darkness; you showed me what it looks like to win my Goddess. Thank you for sneaking money into my cash app when I didn't even ask, but needed desperately! Thank you for answering the call to your gift of dream interpretation. Because if it were not for you, I would have missed the most important messages sent to me by my guides trying to tell me that all I've died and been reborn for was coming, and that my journey was not in vain. My ancestors trusted you to guide me through my dreams mama. I'm glad it was you! Thank you for allowing me to come through you in this lifetime to fulfill my purpose cause I ain't coming back!

To Mark, the man: You have supported me in ways I didn't even know I had room in my heart for. You've shown me pure love, like a father would his daughter. Thank you for showing up.

Activate

To my brother, William, aka Broham: Thank you for being my sounding board when I was losing my mind. I confided in you about things that would scare most people, but it never scared you; In fact, you made sure to validate my crazy. I freaking love you for that!

To my former landlords, Erica and Marcus Maddox: Thank you for allowing me to skip a month's rent when I was fighting for my mother's freedom. I didn't even ask for it, but you saw my fight from an online post and wow! You simply gave a damn about it and about me. Your grace was a reminder that all was not lost. ***THANK YOU!***

To Mr. Lovell, the best numerologist on planet earth: Thank you for actually being *the left* side of my brain when I was in the dark. Because of your support and friendship, I was able to real-eyes my gifts. When I was in the great beyond floating amongst the galaxies, I would call out to you for your ancient insight, and you always answered my calls. Thank you!

To my sister from another Myra: Thank you for being a true friend to me and my family. You stood with us when others turned away. You would sit on the floor with me till the wee hours of the morning, sending out emails, writing letters to human rights activists, and meditating with me for my mother's freedom. I will never forget your true friendship and sisterhood. Thank you.

To Lavetta a.k.a. "V": You filled in the gaps of our lives as a friend and as a sister from another. Your loyalty to those you love is true and unmatched, and I'm grateful for having shared space and time with you. Thank you for having our backs, for your support, and our deep "out of the blue" talks.

To Sahuel: Whenever I would call and say "*I need a meditation session*," you always, always, always opened your doors to me. You never allowed me to feel pity for myself while I was descending into darkness. Thank you for inviting me into your love, and sweat lodges to release any and all that may have been standing in the way of my greatest self. You are my friend, my sister, and confidant.

To Paul Butler (aka White Gold Eagle): Thank you for channeling messages for and from the collective for the 144,000. Every word spoken through your YouTube channel provided deeper insight for me on my journey through the darkness. It was as if the divine would climb out through your videos and wrap its arms around me. THANK YOU, for answering the call.

Activate

Timmesha Burgess

ABOUT THE AUTHOR

TIMMÉSHA BURGESS, was born with a veil—a phenomenon in which babies were both feared and revered, known for having psychic powers, seen as future Dalai Lamas, being mystics, and believed to be reincarnated monarchs and witches. However; other cultures consider this rare birth sighting to be the sign of a child who would rise to become a vampire after death, or transform into a werewolf. Well, she does love to howl and dance naked under full moons; so you never know! However, if you are on this unorthodox journey in this new-age; you'd know better and you'd do your own research as to why certain powers were taught to be feared and suppressed as opposed to exercised wisely. She... like most women and girls, suffered extreme levels of depression and anxiety in her childhood and adult life; and both seemed to increase as she aged. Until she realized the truth behind what they really are, and why they showed up for her. Truths that have been vilified, demonized, and hidden away in secret scrolls… until now!

Timmesha was intuitively led to go on an internal- spiritual journey after sinking in the deep darkness of anxiety and depression herself. A journey she says, only a few survive, and she is one of the few. She earned her Bachelors of Sociology from Lagrange College in 2007, then relocated to Phoenix, AZ, where she later earned her Masters of Science in General Psychology from Grand Canyon University in 2014. After hitting rock bottom after rock bottom moments and struggling to find her own way through life's challenges, she thought to herself several times, "Why am I alive, why was I even born?" In asking these types of questions you get the usual response of "you're depressed"! She became tired of what statistics claimed anxiety, depression, and suicidal thoughts to be; so, she dedicated her life's work to unlocking their hidden messages. Which in-turn orchestrated her odyssey to redefining mental disorders. Only to discover that what she thought was pain for herself and many others; were actually the byproducts of suppressed talents, skills, abilities, and individual superpowers screaming to be unleashed.

REFERENCES

1. Blomquist, Travis Lisa. *Rehabilitating the Witch: The Literary Representation of the Witch from the Malleus Maleficarum to Les Enfants du sabbat.* Rice University.

2. Molnar BE, Berkman LF, Buka SL. "Psychopathology, Childhood Sexual Abuse and Other Childhood Adversities: Relative Links to Subsequent Suicidal Behaviour in the US." Psychol Med. 2001 (31:965-977) [PubMed] [Google Scholar].

3. Harvard T.H. Chan School of Public Health. "Sexual Assault, Harassment Linked with Long-Term Health Problems in Women."

4. The Shamnic Astrology Mystery School. "The Magic of the Number Thirteen" Shamanic Astrology Mystery School. https://shamanicastrology.com/archives/3256.

5. Multhauf, P. Robert. Alchemy. "Pseudoscience. Alchemy - The Chemistry of Alchemy." Britannica. https://www.britannica.com/topic/alchemy/The-chemistry-of-alchemy./

6. Yalcinalp, Esra. "Turkey Erdogan: Women rise up over withdrawal from Istanbul Convention." BBC News. https://www.bbc.com/news/world-europe-56516462.

7. Verywellhealth.com. "Disease or Disorder. Disease or Disorder: What Is the Difference?" verywellhealth.com.

8. Jung, Carl. "Psychology and Alchemy - Exploring your mind." *Psychology Today.* https://exploringyourmind.com/carl-jung-psychology-and-alchemy/

9. Gupta, Shubhra. "Bulbbul movie review: A Powerfully Feminist, Revisionist Tale." https://indianexpress.com/article/entertainment/movie-review/bulbbul-movie-review-rahul-bose-6473779/.

10. Mark, Joshua. "Jezebel." https://en.wikipedia.org/wiki/Jessabelle.2020.

11. Learn the six plant growth. Safer Brand. Stages. https://www.saferbrand.com/articles/plant-growth-stages

12. Petkova, Marina. "The Mystery of the Black Madonna." 2020. https://historyofyesterday.com/the-mystery-of-the-black-madonna-a0503c5f537

13. "Never Give Up." https://www.reddit.com/r/bonehurtingjuice/comments/d0xd38/never_dont_give_up/.

14. Pookrum, Jewel. "The Truth About Disease & States of Consciousness." https://www.youtube.com/watch?v=niwRAs_X-ss. 1994.

www.ingramcontent.com/pod-product-compliance
Lightning Source LLC
Chambersburg PA
CBHW051425290426
44109CB00016B/1434